Capital Gains Tax

Capital Gains Tax

Eighth Edition

Bill Pritchard, BA, FTII

Pitman

PITMAN PUBLISHING
128 Long Acre, London WC2E 9AN

©Longman Group UK Ltd 1985

First published in Great Britain 1972
This edition 1987

British Library Cataloguing in Publication Data

Pritchard, W.E.
  Capital gains tax.—8th ed.
  1. Capital gains tax—Great Britain
  I. Title
  336.24'3   HJ4707

ISBN 0-7121 0763 0

All rights reserved. No part of this publication may be reproduced,
stored in a retrieval system, or transmitted, in any form or by any
means, electronic, mechanical, photocopying, recording and/or
otherwise without the prior written permission of the publishers.
This book may not be lent, resold, hired out or otherwise disposed
of by way of trade in any form of binding or cover other than that
in which it is published, without the prior consent of the publishers.

Printed and bound in Great Britain

Contents

	Preface	
Chapter One	General Aspects	1
Chapter Two	The Charge to Tax and Administration	3
Chapter Three	Chargeable Persons	6
Chapter Four	Individuals	8
Chapter Five	Settled Property	14
Chapter Six	Companies	19
Chapter Seven	Chargeable Assets	24
Chapter Eight	Chargeable Occasions	38
Chapter Nine	Rules of Computation	44
Chapter Ten	General Relief for Gifts	64
Chapter Eleven	Losses	68
Chapter Twelve	Assets Restored or Replaced	71
Chapter Thirteen	Value Shifting	75
Chapter Fourteen	Stocks and Shares	76
Chapter Fifteen	Various Exemptions	115
Chapter Sixteen	Transfer of a Business to a Company	117
Chapter Seventeen	Replacement of Business Assets	122
Chapter Eighteen	Gift of Business Assets	127
Chapter Nineteen	Transfer of a Business on Retirement	130
Chapter Twenty	Business Assets − Miscellaneous Matters	138
Chapter Twenty One	Interests in Land	143
Chapter Twenty Two	Development Land Tax	147
Chapter Twenty Three	Leases	148
Chapter Twenty Four	Purchase of Own Shares by Unquoted Trading Company	159
Chapter Twenty Five	The Anti-Avoidance Legislation	166
Chapter Twenty Six	Foreign Matters	167
Chapter Twenty Seven	Further revision questions	169
	Index	178

Preface

This book is a companion volume to "Income Tax" and "Corporation tax". It is intended for professional students taking final examinations.

At the end of most chapters are revision questions with answers for the use of students, and at the end of the book are further example with answers in a separate answer book. These latter examples are for the use of lecturers who wish to set homework. To help students using the book for private study, only the answer to every alternate question is given at the end of the questions.

The book incorporates the provisions of the Finance Acts, 1987.

W.E. Pritchard
September, 1987.

Chapter One

General Aspects

Introduction

Before 1965 most types of capital gains were exempted from taxation apart from the isolated type which was brought within the charge of income tax either by a specific piece of legislation or because they were defined by the courts as "adventures in the nature of trade" (see the tax cases on: CIR v CAPE BRANDY SYNDICATE regarding a sale of brandy; ST. AUBYN ESTATES LTD. v HARRIS (STC 159) regarding the sale of a landed estate).

But apart from these isolated cases, the first attempt at producing a capital gains tax came in the Finance Act 1962. This created a new Case VII of Schedule D which assessed a selection of capital gains to income tax. The creation of the full capital gains tax was left to Part III of the Finance Act, 1965.

Case VII only applied to short term capital gains, which were basically those with less than twelve months between the relevant acquisition and the chargeable disposal of the asset. Capital gains tax applies to all gains where Case VII was not applicable. Thus capital gains tax could be applied to a gain where the period between purchase and sale was less than twelve months but for some reason Case VII was invalid.

Case VII was abolished as from April 6th 1971 and capital gains tax applies to all chargeable disposals arising on or after that date.

In 1979 the legislation (apart from that relating to companies) was consolidated in the Capital Gains Taxes Act, 1979 (normally referred to as the CGTA, 1979) and all references to the legislation in the book are to that Act unless otherwise stated. The relevant legislation for companies is contained in the Taxes Act, 1970.

General

As its name implies, capital gains tax is a tax on capital profits — on the profits made on the disposal of capital assets. Before it can be decided what tax is payable, several questions have to be answered:

1. Who is liable to pay tax? Most legal persons (individuals, companies, trusts, etc.) are liable, but there are certain exceptions.

2 General Aspects

2. What assets are included? Most assets are included whether they have physical presence (e.g. buildings) or not (e.g. shares). Again there are certain assets on the disposal of which no tax is payable.

3. When is there a "disposal" on which a liability can arise? This includes occasions other than sales e.g. gifts, destruction of an asset, etc.

4. The gain is generally the difference in the sale price (or market value) and:

a) Costs of acquisition and improvement

b) Incidental costs of purchase and sale.

Since 6th April, 1982 the allowable expenditure can be increased to take account of the effects of inflation as measured by the Retail Price Index.

5. Are losses allowable? Yes, but with restrictions in certain circumstances.

6. At what rate is the tax assessed? This varies.

This books attempts to answer these questions.

References to section numbers are to the Capital Gains Taxes Act, 1979 unless otherwise stated. Other references to Acts are:

1. TMA, 1970 which is the Taxes Management Act, 1970.

2. FA, 1980 which is the Finance Act 1980 (or whatever year is relevant).

Chapter Two

The Charge to Tax and Administration

The charge to tax (Ss 1 and 2)

Capital gains tax is assessed on a person who is resident or ordinarily resident in the United Kingdom on the disposal of a chargeable asset.

A subject of the United Kingdom is thus liable to the tax on the disposal of an asset anywhere in the world so long as he is resident or ordinarily resident in the United Kingdom at the time of the disposal. A foreigner will be assessed on the disposal of assets in the United Kingdom if resident here. If he is resident here and disposes of assets abroad, he is only liable on the amount of the gain remitted to this country.

A person is also liable on gains made in a year he is not resident or ordinarily resident, but is carrying on a trade in the UK through a branch or agency. The gains assessable are, however, restricted to those made on assets held in the UK for the purposes of the trade and/or the branch or agency. (S.12(1)(2)).

The rate of charge is 30% of the total gain with differences for individuals and companies.

The assessment is on a current year basis, i.e. the basis period in the tax year itself. For example, for tax year 1980/81 the capital gains assessment is on all gains less losses (brought forward and of the current year) made between 6th April, 1980 and 5th April, 1981.

Responsibility for administration

The tax is the direct responsibility of the Commissioners of Inland Revenue together with most other forms of direct taxation. Local Inspectors compute and assess the amount of tax payable and the Collector's Branch is responsible for collection.

Returns

Capital gains are normally included in the annual income tax return which generally require a return of all gains for the preceding year. Special returns can be issued by the Inspector if required, but this is rarely done in practice.

4   **The Charge to Tax and Administration**

However, on completing the tax returns for 1980/81 onwards individuals need not enter the exact details of the chargeable gains if they are less than the annual exemption limit and the total of the disposal proceeds does not exceed twice the annual exemption. Normally a statement that gains and receipts do not exceed these limits is all that is needed (S.5(5)).

Details of any acquisition of capital assets in the year with dates and prices, can also be requested.

Partners are treated as individuals, but partnership returns must include disposals and acquisitions by partnerships.

Assessments

Assessments are not normally made until the year end, but in cases such as death or the winding up of a trust, when liability is known and has been agreed before the year end, can be made before the end of the year.

Appeals

The usual rights of appeal against an assessment exist. The taxpayer can appeal to the General or Special Commissioners except when the valuation of land is in dispute, when the case is heard by the appropriate Lands Tribunal. (S.31 and S.47, TMA 70).

Appeals or questions of value of unquoted shares arising on or after 13th March, 1975 are heard only by the Special Commissioners (S.47(3), TMA, 70).

Payment of the tax

Capital gains tax is payable (from 1980/81) on or before 1st December following the year of assessment after the end of the relevant year of assessment, or thirty days after the issue of the assessment whichever is the later. (S.7). For 1979/80 and earlier years the tax was payable on 6th July following the year of assessment.

The rules about interest on unpaid tax apply as for income tax.

In certain circumstances, the tax can be recovered from person other than the one assessed:

1. Tax assessed on trustees can sometimes be recovered from the beneficiaries. (S.52(4)).

2. If liability arises on a gift, and the donor does not pay, the recipient can be assessed at any time within two years of the date the tax was payable by the donor. The donee can recover the tax from the donor. (S.59).

The Charge to Tax and Administration 5

Capital gains tax is normally payable in one sum, but instalment payments are available. In other cases, if the taxpayer can show hardship would arise by paying the tax in one sum, he can apply to the Board of Inland Revenue to pay by instalments. The Board can allow what instalments they feel are appropriate, but in no case must the period of payment exceed eight years (S.40(1)).

Chapter Three

General

Liability

For all practical purposes, those assessable to capital gains tax can be divided into three groups: (2(1)):
1. Individuals, including partnerships.
2. Trustees.
3. Companies.

A person must be resident or ordinarily resident in the United Kingdom to be charged to capital gains tax, except when carrying on a business here. A husband and wife can have separate status for this purpose.

When a person is resident or ordinarily resident in the UK but not of UK domicile, gains on the disposal of overseas assets are only assessed on any part of the gains remitted to this country.

Residence, ordinary residence, and domicile have the same meanings as for income tax.

A partnership is not a person for the purposes of capital gains tax. Gains accruing on the disposal of partnership assets are apportioned among the partners in accordance with the share of the partnership assets under the terms of the agreement and assessed on each partner individually. A disposal of an interest in a partnership is not a disposal of a chargeable asset as such. It is a disposal of an interest in assets some of which are chargeable, and some of which are not. (S.60)).

Exempted persons
Under S.145, CGTA, 1979, the following are exempted:
1. Charities as long as the gains are used for charitable purposes.
2. Superannuation funds approved by the Inland Revenue.
3. Registered friendly societies.
4. Scientific research associations.
5. Local authorities.
6. Diplomatic representatives.

Rate of tax

The rate payable is 30% for individuals and trustees. Companies pay corporation tax at the appropriate company rate.

For individuals and trusts, there are reliefs available which may reduce the charge in the form of exemption for gains below a certain amount.

Chapter Four

Individuals

General (Sch. 1)

Individuals are assessable to capital gains tax on net gains made in a particular year, but they are entitled to special relief on the amount of tax payable. These reliefs also apply to:

1. Trustees for the mentally disabled and those in receipt of attendance allowance.

2. The personal representatives of a deceased person for the year of death and the two following years.

The annual exemption (for 1987/88) is the first £6,600 of gains, any balance being charged at 30%.

Example

1. For 1987/88 Charles Ponsonby makes net gains of £10,000 and losses of £1,000. The capital gains position is:

Gross gains	10,000
Losses	(1,000)
Net gains	9,000
Annual exemption	(6,600)
Tax payable on	2,400×30%
Tax payable =	720
(On or by 1, December, 1988)	

Special rates of tax and reliefs are also available to trustees of settlements and companies, but these are dealt with in detail in later chapters.

Losses

As is discussed in detail later in the book, it is possible to make a loss on a disposal and losses can be offset against chargeable gains of the same year and any excess loss carried forward and offset against chargeable gains of future years. In calculating the charge to tax on individuals two rules should be remembered about losses:

Individuals 9

1. Losses of the current year are offset first and in full against gains of the current year even if this reduces the net gains below the annual exemption level.

2. Losses brought forward are only utilized to the extent needed to reduce the net chargeable gains to the annual exemption limit (£6,600 for 1987/88).

Example
Joe Farnsbarns has these results:
1986/87:

Losses for the year		(3,950)
Gains for the year		2,000
Unused losses carried forward		(1,950)

1987/88:

Gains for the year		8,300
Losses in the year		(1,300)
		7,000
Losses brought forward	(1,950)	
Utilized	400	(400)
Carry forward	1,550	
Net gain (wholly covered by the annual exemption)		6,600

Husband and wife

Disposals between a husband and wife are exempt (S.44). They are ignored in calculating the exemption and reliefs, but disposals by *both* are included in calculating whether gains in a year are above or below the annual exemption.

Example
For 1987/88 Mr. Bliss makes chargeable gains of £6,000 and Mrs. Bliss chargeable gains of £2,400.

Tax payable by the couple:		
Total gains:	$6{,}000+2{,}400=$	8,400
Charged:		
	$6{,}600\times\text{Nil}=$	Nil
	$1{,}800\times30\%=$	540
	8,400	540

However, in the year of marriage each is treated as a separate individual and the reliefs, etc. are therefore applied separately to each, e.g. there is relief, etc. if each makes individual gains of less than the annual exemption.

10 Individuals

When an election has been made for separate assessment, any exemption, reduced rate or marginal relief is apportioned between them in proportion to the amount of their liabilities as if no relief, etc. were in operation i.e. in proportion to their net chargeable gains.

Losses

The losses of husband and wife for a year are set primarily against that person's gain, any excess then being carried over to the spouse. Losses brought forward are similarly treated. Thus the losses of a married couple are interchangeable unless they elect not to be so treated.

Example

Joe and Maggie Nagg have these results:

1986/87:	**Joe**		**Maggie**	
Losses	(2,200)	Gains		2,400
Gains	700	Losses		(1,800)
Unused loss	(1,500)	Net gains		600
Offset against spouse's gains	600			(600)
Unused loss carried forward	(900)			Nil

1987/88:	**Joe**		**Maggie**	
Gains	8,600	Gains		4,000
Losses	(200)	Losses		(4,300)
	8,400	Unused losses		(300)
Loss of year offset	(300)			300
	8,100			Nil
Losses brought forward	(900)			
	7,200			
Annual exemption	6,600			
	600	$\times\ 30\% =\ 180.00$		

An election, which must be made before 6, July, following the end of the year of assessment can be made to have the gains of husband and wife separately assessed. This means the tax payable remains the same generally, but the wife is legally responsible for paying her share. If the election is made the losses of husband and wife are kept separate which can be an advantage if current year losses would be otherwise wasted by reducing the spouse's gains below the annual exemption level (S.45).

11 Individuals

Example

A husband and wife have these results in 1987/88:

Husband losses of		(1,600)
Wife gains of		6,700
Without any election:		
Wife's gains		6,700
Husband's losses	(1,600)	
Losses offset	1,600	(1,600)
	Nil	
Net gain		5,100
If the election was made:		
Wife's gains		6,700
Husband's losses	(1,600)	
Unused losses carried forward	(1,600)	
Gain		6,700
Annual exemption		6,600
		100 × 30%
		= 30.00

An election remains in force until withdrawn within the same time limits.

As previously mentioned, inter-spouse transfers do not lead to assessable gains or allowable losses. However, such transfers are affected by the rules of indexation in that on an inter-spouse transfer, the base cost has to be increased by an indexation allowance if appropriate to calculate the acquisition value of the recipient spouse.

Example

Fred Smythe acquired a property for £20,000 in August, 1978. He gave it to his wife in October, 1985 when it was worth £40,000. She sold it in February, 1988 for £42,000.

Disposal by Fred:		
Original cost		20,000
Indexation allowance (say)		1,700
Deemed acquisition value of wife		21,700
Sale of wife		42,000
Acquisition value	21,700	
Indexation allowance (say)	500	22,200
Gain		19,800

In a year of separation or death of the husband, the annual exemption is available to the wife in full in respect of gains arising during the remainder of the same fiscal year. This does *not* apply to the man in the year of his wife's death or a separation.

12 **Individuals**

Personal representatives/executors of deceased person (S.48 & para. 4, Sch.1)

When an individual dies his personal representatives acquire the assets (for capital gains purposes) at their market value on the date of death.

Any disposals to beneficiaries are not an occasion of charge. This only happens if they sell assets. If so they qualify for the same annual exemption as an individual for the remainder of the year of death (but a *full* annual exemption — there is no apportionment) and the two following years.

The subject is dealt with in more detail in chapter 9.

Revision questions

1. Joseph and Mary Green have these transactions in 1987/88.
   a) Work out their liability to capital gains tax assuming no elections are made.
   b) What would be the situation if an election were made for separate assessment?

Joseph	Losses brought forward from 1986/87	(1,600)
	Gains in 1987/88	7,700
	Losses in 1987/88	(500)
Mary	Gain in 1987/88	400
	Losses in 1987/88	(2,200)

2. George Holden bought a property in 1978 for £20,000 and transferred it to his wife Joan in December, 1983, when it was worth £48,000. She sold it in July, 1987 for £60,000. The value at 31st March, 1982 was £30,000.

Assume Retail Price Index figures as follows:

March, 1982	79.44
December, 1983	86.89
July, 1985	110.00

Answers

1.a)	**Joseph**			**Mary**		
Gains		7,700	Gains			400
Losses of 1987/88	(500)		Losses of 1985/86	(2,200)	
Offset	500	(500)	Offset	400	(400)
	Nil	7,200		(1,800)	Nil
Offset Mary's Losses		1,800		1,800	
		5,400 C/F		Nil	

Losses B/F from 1986/87 (1,600), C/F to 1988/89. Gain exempt, less than £6,600.

13 Individuals

b)

Joseph			Mary		
Gains		7,700	Gains		400
Losses of 1987/88	(500)		Losses of 1987/88	(2,200)	
Offset	500	(500)	Offset	400	(400)
	Nil	7,200	C/F to 1988/89	(1,800)	Nil
Losses B/F					
from 1986/87	(1,600)				
Offset	600	(600)			
C/F to 1988/89	(1,000)	6,600			

2. Disposal from George to Joan:

Cost in 1978	20,000

Indexation allowance $30,000 \times \dfrac{86.89-79.44}{79.44} =$ 2,820

(0.094)

Deemed acquisition value of Joan	22,820

No capital gain − transfer between spouses.
Disposal by Mary:

Sale price		60,000
Acquisition	22,820	

Indexation allowance $22,820 \times \dfrac{110-86.89}{86.89} =$ 6,071   28,891

(0.266)   Gain   31,109

Chapter Five

Settled Property

General

"Settled property" is defined as any property held in trust other than property held by a person as nominee or as bare trustee . A trust is a legal device by which certain property is entrusted to the care of a person (trustee) who has to deal with it in certain ways for the benefit of other persons (beneficiaries).

When a person is absolutely entitled to an asset which is administered on his behalf by nominees or bare trustees, those nominees or bare trustees are not treated as having a separate existence from the owner for capital gains purposes. Their actions are taken to be synonymous with those of the owner, and therefore any capital gain arising on disposal by the bare trustees, etc. is a gain of the owner.

There are three persons affected by capital gains tax in connection with trusts:
1. The settlor.
2. The trustees.
3. The beneficiaries.

The settlor

There is a disposal of property by the settlor on any transfer of property to trustees, and therefore any liability is personal to the settlor. The whole property comprised in the settlement is deemed to be disposed of whether or not the gift is irrecoverable or the settlor retains any interest in the settlement (S.29A).

A settlor and trustees are "connected persons" and therefore market value of the property at the date the settlement is created is taken as the disposal value (S.62 & 63 and Berry v. Warnett (1980 STC 631)).

The gifts rollover relief has been extended to include gifts in settlement. The donor can make the necessary election unilaterally (S.78, FA, 1981). Under the relief the trustees take over the base cost of the donor, increased by an indexation allowance, if appropriate. The trustees then have to retain the asset for over twelve months before a further indexation allowance can apply.

Trustees

Occasions of charge

The rules regarding trustees have been considerably altered as from 6, April, 1982.

There is an occasion of charge, as there always has been, when trustees sell assets at arm's length.

When a life interest terminates (S.84, FA, 1982):

1. And such a termination means a beneficiary becomes absolutely entitled to the property as against the trustees, there is an occasion of charge.

2. When a life interest terminates on the death of a life tenant:

a) And the property continues to be settled property, or someone becomes absolutely entitled, there is no chargeable occasion, and the property is deemed to be sold and re-acquired at its then market value, but there is no chargeable gain or allowable loss.

b) If the life interest is only in part of the property, then all necessary apportionments are made.

3. When the settlor elected to rollover his accumulated gain on setting up the trust, it can be recovered on any subsequent death of a life tenant. The remainder of any deemed gain is not assessable. When the life tenant has only an interest in part only of the trust property, all necessary apportionments have to be made.

Example

R settles £27,000 of assets on P for life and then to J absolutely. R rolls over a gain of £7,000 to the trustees who thus have a deemed acquisition value of £20,000. On P's death the assets have a value of £45,000 (the value at which J acquires them), but the trustees are assessed on a gain of £7,000.

Gifts relief (S.82, FA, 1982)

For transfers by trustees from 6, April, 1982 they can, in a joint election with the recipient, apply the gifts rollover relief to any gain accruing to the trustees.

As under the other applications of gifts relief, any CTT or inheritance tax paid on the original transfer can be added to the acquisition value of the transferee, but it cannot convert a gain to a loss.

Losses

When trustees transfer an asset to a beneficiary absolutely, any allowable loss attaching to the property which the trustees have not utilized can be transferred to the beneficiary. It is immaterial whether the loss accrued in the year of transfer or was brought forward.

16 **Settled Property**

Example
Martin died in 1979 and left two properties to his wife Mabel for life. Their acquisition values to the trustees were:

Apex House	100,000
Base House	90,000

On Mabel's death the properties passed to the sons absolutely, Apex House going to Joe and Base House to Fred. Their values at the time:

Apex House	110,000
Base House	120,000

The loss situation is:

Base House – value	120,000	Apex House – value		110,000
Acquisition value		Acquisition value	100,000	
Say, no indexation	90,000	Indexation allowance (say)	3,000	103,000
Loss	(30,000)	Gain		7,000
Loss offset	7,000			(7,000)
Unused loss	(23,000)			Nil

Joe therefore acquires Apex House at a value of £110,000 and Fred Base House at a value of £120,000 with an unrelieved loss of (£23,000).

Tax payable by trustees

Trustees qualify for an annual exemption of half the amount allowed to individuals (£3,300 for 1987/88) (Para.5, Sch.1). For settlements ("qualifying settlements") created on or after 6, June, 1978, which have the same settlor (and are defined therefore as forming a "group") the annual exemption is divided equally among the settlements in the group, with a maximum apportioned exemption of one tenth.

Trustees need only return gains in detail if, in a year, they exceed their annual exemption (£3,300 for 1987/88) and/or their total disposal values are twice the trustees' exemption limit (£6,600 for 1987/88).

If tax assessed on trustees is not paid by them within six months of the due date and the asset (or any sale proceeds) is transferred to any absolutely beneficiary, he can be made to pay the trustees' liability. The assessment on the beneficiary must be made within two years of the due date of the trustees (S.52(4)).

Beneficiaries (S.58)

There is no chargeable gain on the disposal of an interest by a beneficiary (e.g. life tenant, annuitant, remainderman, etc.) except when he acquired the interest for cash or moneys worth.

There is a chargeable occasion, however, if a beneficiary who has acquired an interest in possession becomes absolutely entitled to the trust assets.

Settled Property 17

This is also on occasion of charge on the trustees. This only seems to bring a charge on the beneficiary when a life tenant acquires the reversionary interest, and not when the remainderman acquires a life interest.

Revision question

Mr. Hills has made heaps of money in his lifetime. In August, 1982 he settles a block of shares in Apex Enterprises plc on trust for his grandchild Egbert. He acquired the shares for £30,000 in 1979. On transfer to the trustees they are worth £52,000. The trustees paid £3,000 capital transfer tax on the gift.

In January, 1983 the trustees sell 25% of the shares for £16,000.

In September, 1983 they distribute the remainder of the shares to Egbert absolutely. They are then worth £90,000. Capital transfer tax of £2,000 is paid.

In October, 1987 Egbert sells them for £103,000.

Assume Retail Price Index:

March, 1982		79.44
August, 1982		81.90
January, 1983		82.61
August, 1983		85.68
September, 1983		86.06
October, 1984	(say)	112.00

Calculate the capital gains tax payable on each transfer, assuming no other transactions by anyone.

Answer

Assuming Mr. Hill made a gifts relief rollover election (the trustees are not a party to it) there would be no gain on Hill, and the acquisition value of the trustees would be:

Cost to Hill	30,000
Indexation allowance $30,000 \times \dfrac{81.90 - 79.44}{79.44} = (0.031)$	930
	30,930
CTT paid	3,000
	33,930

Sale by trustees:	
Sale price	16,000
Cost* $33,930 \times 25\% =$	(8,483)
Gain	7,517
Exemption	(2,500)
	$5,017 \times 30\% =$
	1,015.10

*No indexation allowance, as not held by trustees for over twelve months.

18   Settled Property

Distribution to Egbert:
No disposal by trustees (assuming gifts relief election by them).

Cost to Egbert:	33,930
Written off	8,483
	25,447

$$\text{Indexation } 25,447 \times \frac{86.06 - 85.68}{85.68} \ (0.005) = 128*$$

	25,675

Sale by Egbert:

Sale price		103,000
Cost	25,675	

$$\text{Indexation allowance } 25,675 \times \frac{112 - 86.06}{86.06} \ (0.301) = 7,728$$

	(33,403)
	69,597
Exemption	(6,600)
	62,997

$$62,997 \times 30\% = 18.899.10$$

*Before April 1985 only indexed from 12 months after acquisition.

Trustees or Assignees in Bankruptcy

(S.61)

When a man goes bankrupt, his assets are taken over by a trustee or assignee in bankruptcy who is then responsible for the paying off of the debts of the bankrupt.

There is no disposal of assets on the takeover of the bankrupt's assets by the trustee of assignee. His position is that of a nominee or bare trustee against whom the debtor is absolutely entitled to any assets. Transactions between them are disregarded. If a trustee disposes of any assets tax is assessable as if the bankrupt had disposed of them, but the tax is assessed on that paid by the trustee.

If the bankrupt dies, the assets held by the trustee at death are treated as held by him as the personal representative and the special rules applying to personal representatives apply to the trustee.

Chapter Six

Companies

Profits

The profits of companies, which include both income and capital gains, are assessable to corporation tax. Thus, a company is not liable to capital gains tax as such, but pays corporation tax at an appropriate percentage rate on any gains it makes. The gains are computed according to the normal rules of capital gains tax. (S.238, TA, 1970).

It has been proposed the method of taxing capital gains on companies be changed from 17th March, 1987, but the implementation of these changes may be delayed because of the 1987 general election.

Any capital gains made in a chargeable accounting period are first of all set off against capital losses of the same period or unused losses brought forward.

The net gains, if made before 17th March, 1987 were then reduced to a fraction. Trading losses of the same or succeeding accounting periods could then be offset against the reduced gains. The net gains were then charged at the then existing standard rate of corporation tax, giving an effective rate of charge of 30%. No advance corporation tax could be utilized against the tax charged on the capital gains.

Example
In year ended 31st March, 1986 a company made a capital gain of £40,000 and a capital loss of £10,000. A trading loss of £6,000 was also to be offset against the net gains. The standard rate of corporation tax was 40%. Appropriate fraction for company capital gains was 3/4.

Gross gain	40,000	
Capital loss	(10,000)	
	30,000 $\times$ ¾ =	22,500
Offset trade loss		(6,000)
		16,500

$$16,500 \times 40\% = 6,600$$

20 Companies

Finance Bill, 1987
For gains made from 17th March, 1987 it was proposed in the original 1987 Finance Bill to:
1. Offset capital gains against capital losses as before.
2. Then offset appropriate trade losses (without reducing the net gains to a fraction).
3. Then include the remaining gains as part of the chargeable income of the company.
4. Charge the gains as part of the income at the appropriate rate of corporation tax (small company, marginal rate or standard rate).
5. If appropriate, set advance corporation tax against the corporation tax charge on the capital gain.

Example
A company in an accounting period made a trading profit of 100,000 and a capital gain of 20,000 and paid a dividend of 70,000.

It is assumed the marginal rate limits are 100,000 and 500,000, the basic rate of income tax 27% and the standard rate of corporation tax 35%, and the marginal relief fraction 1/50.

$$
\begin{array}{ll}
\text{Sch.D, Case I} & 100,000 \\
\text{Capital gain} & \underline{20,000} \\
& 120,000 \times 35\% = 42,000
\end{array}
$$

Marginal relief:
$$
(500,000 - 120,000) \times \frac{120,000}{120,000} \times \frac{1}{50} = \quad \begin{array}{r}(7,600) \\ \hline 34,400\end{array}
$$

ACT offset:
$$
70,000 \times \frac{27}{73} = \quad (25,890)
$$

MCT payable $\qquad \underline{\underline{8,510}}$

Exemption
The annual exemption is not available to companies which must pay tax at the relevant percentage rate of corporation tax. There is an exception for a company holding funds in a fiduciary capacity and generally this means holding the investments of its own employees' superannuation fund. Any gains on the sale of these assets are exempted from tax if the fund is approved by the Inland Revenue. If it is not approved, or is not wholly approved, liability can arise on the disposal of assets of the unapproved portion.

Companies 21

Transfer of assets between members of a group

In a group of companies within common ownership, no gain arises on an inter-group transfer of assets. However, there is a gain computed when an asset leaves the group. The gain is calculated as the difference between the disposal price and the price paid on acquisition by a group member, irrespective of whether that company was the owner on sale. If the original acquisition was before 6th April, 1965, that date is taken for the calculation of the time apportionment formula. There are certain occasions when this general rule does not apply and the disposal gives rise to tax.(S.273(2), *I* and *CTA*,70).

These exceptions are:

1. When a debt is paid off.
2. The redemption of shares.
3. A disposal of an interest in shares on a capital distribution.
4. A receipt of compensation for damage to an asset.

When assets have had capital allowances granted on them, any loss on sale is restricted for capital gains purposes. For an asset used within a group, all capital allowances granted to members of the group on the particular asset are included, even when the company owning the asset leaves the group — see below. (*S.* 275(1), *I* and *CTA*, 70).

In computing "rollover" relief (see later) under *S.*33. all the trades carried on by a group are treated as one trade, thus ensuring the relief is available on intergroup transfers. (*S.*276, *I* and *CTA*, 70).

A group of companies for tax purposes can generally only include UK residents. A company is resident in the place its central control and management are situated.

A group of companies has a principal and subsidiary companies, a "subsidiary" for capital gains tax being a company in which the principal company owns directly or indirectly at least 75% of the ordinary share capital. (*S.*272(1),*ICTA*, 70).

Company ceasing to be a member of a group

The Finance Act, 1968 introduced legislation whereby when a group member leaves there is a relevant disposal of all the assets it has received from other group members. The company leaving the group is generally liable for the tax but the Revenue have powers of recovery from its former fellow members in any case of non- payment.The gain is the difference between market value on the date the company acquired the asset, minus the original group purchase price. (*S.*278). This section applies only where the asset was acquired within six years of the company leaving the group.

When a subsidiary company leaves a group after its shares have been the subject of an exchange during the course of a group reconstruction, there is no longer

22 Companies

an automatic charge to tax, (as there was to reconstructions taking place prior to 19th April, 1977 if the subsidiary left the group within six years (S.279, TA, 1970). This six year rule still applies to reconstructions prior to 19th April, 1977, so only expired on 18th April, 1983). Now, "degrouping" for bona fide commercial reasons does not normally entail a charge to tax.

S.280 stops a situation in which a loss to offset a gain is artificially created by a group manoeuvre known as a depreciatory transfer: parent company A has two subsidiaries B and C. The only asset of B is a freehold property. A purchased B's shares for £5,000. In an accounting period A makes a capital gain of £2,000 and wishes to offset this with a loss. This is accomplished by selling B's property to C for £3,000 (when the market value is £8,000) and later all the shares in B (which A owns) are sold for £3,000, which is all they are worth, B's only asset being a bank account of £3,000. The loss can be disallowed "as not being just or reasonable having regard to the depreciatory transfer". This section does not apply if the dividend stripping legislation is relevant. (S.280,ICTA,70).

The above provisions do not apply if a company which has acquired an asset from another group member, leaves the group as part of a bona fide merger without tax avoidance being one of the main objectives. There are conditions as to what is a "merger" and the proportion of shares which must be taken over. (S.278A).

Transfer of assets on a company reconstruction (S.267).

When a company disposes of the whole or part of its business to another company as part of a scheme of reconstruction or amalgamation, no chargeable gain arises on the disposal because it is deemed to be sold for such a price as gives rise to neither gain or loss.

Of course, certain conditions have to be satisfied. Both companies must be resident in the UK at the time of transfer, the scheme must involve the transfer of the whole or part of the business to another company, and the transferor must not receive any consideration for the transfer, but the transferee is allowed to take over the whole or part of the liabilities.

Moreover, transfers after 19th April, 1977 are denied relief if the scheme of reconstruction or amalgamation is not a bona fide commercial transaction or forms part of a tax avoidance scheme (S.267(3A)). Clearance may be obtained from the Board on application by the company acquiring the assets.

Assets owned at 6th April, 1965 are deemed to have been acquired by the transferee at the time of their original acquisition by the transferor.

Generally trading stock is not covered by this provision.

Companies 23

Liquidation

On the liquidation of a limited company there are two separate occasions on which capital gains tax arises:

1. Gains or losses accruing to the company on the sale or disposal of its assets by the liquidator.

2. Gains or losses accruing to the shareholders on the repayment of their share capital by the liquidator.

Even if the assets of the company are taken over by the shareholders in specie as payment for the shares, there are two separate chargeable occasions.

During the liquidation, shareholders often receive more than one distribution. Each distribution, other than the final one, is strictly a part disposal by the shareholder, and the residual value of the shares should be ascertained in order to apportion part of the cost to the part disposal.

To get round this difficulty in the case of unquoted companies, the Inland Revenue are prepared to deal with the calculations on a reasonable practical basis. If the liquidation is expected to be completed within two years of the first distribution payment, the Revenue will accept any reasonable estimate of the value of the shares at the date of distributions. If the distributions are completed before any assessment is raised (and normally the Revenue will not raise any assessments for two years) the Revenue are prepared to accept the residual value of the shares in relation to any particular distribution is equal to the actual amount of the subsequent distributions.

Where time apportionment applies, the Revenue are prepared to calculate the gain on each distribution by applying the fraction as at the date of the first distribution without any further adjustment.

If a shareholder has paid income tax on an apportionment of relevant income, and has never had income tax relief, he can add the amount paid to his base cost for capital gains tax purposes on any subsequent disposal such as a liquidation (S.74).

Chapter Seven

Chargeable Assets

General

All forms of property are assets for capital gains tax unless there is a specific exemption. Therefore the following are assets a disposal of which could give rise to a tax liability:

1. Options and debts (but see later) and any form of interest or rights over property.

2. Currency other than sterling. Dealers in currency are normally assessed on their gains under Case 1, Schedule D as a trading profit.

3. Any property created by the person disposing of it or which comes to be owned without being created e.g. leases.

As regards debts these are not generally a chargeable asset apart from a debt on a security. This is dealt with in detail later in the chapter.

Exemptions

There are complete and partial exemptions.

The complete exemptions are:

1. Motor vehicles, of a type commonly used or suitable to be used as private motor vehicles. (S.130).

2. Small gifts not exceeding £100 in total in any one year. Do not confuse this with the similar capital transfer tax rules when the £100 of every gift is automatically exempted. In capital gains gifts in one year are only exempted if the total value of gifts in the year is £100 or less. (S.6).

3. Currency (of any type) for an individual's private use. (S.135).

4. Decorations for valour if acquired otherwise than by purchase. (S.131).

5. Betting and lottery wins. (S.19(4)).

6. Compensation or damages for PERSONAL wrongs or injuries. Compensations for damage to PROPERTY can be assessable (S.19(5).

Chargeable Assets   25

For disposals occurring after 19th December, 1974 of the rights of the insured under a policy of insurance, there is a charge to CGT in so far as the property insured was a chargeable asset. No allowable losses can be established under this provision. (S.140).

7. (a) Chattels (tangible, moveable property) which have an anticipated useful life of fifty years or less (called ''wasting assets'') (S.127). This exemption does not apply if capital allowances were (or could have been) claimed on the chattel.
''Moveable'' means moveable by mechanical means as well as capable of being lifted by an individual.

(b) Chattels are also exempted if the sale price at disposal does not exceed £3,000 (whether or not they are wasting assets). This is dealt with in detail later. (S.128).

8. Life assurance policies or deferred annuities either on maturity or on earlier surrender or sale. If, however, the person making the disposal was not the original beneficial owner of the policy, he would be chargeable on any gain. (S.140).

9. Also exempt are certain disposals if they are conditionally exempt from capital transfer tax (S.147). The items involved are:

(a) Land, buildings, contents of buildings (together with funds for maintenance), works of art and scientific collections given for the public benefit to a non-profit making body, subject to Treasury approval. They may require certain undertaking as to maintenance, public access, etc. (S.147 and S.148).

(b) Works of art, historic buildings, etc. designed by the Treasury of being of national, historic, etc. interest. Any gift (including a gift of settlement) or deemed disposal by trustees is exempt, conditional on certain undertakings being observed. The disposal is deemed to take place at a value so that no gain or loss arises. (S.147).

(c) Gifts to charities. (S.146).

10. (a) Any profit made on various types of non-marketable government saving schemes and securities such as National Savings Certificates, Development Bonds and Premium Bonds. (S.71).

(b) Marketable government securities.

11. Exemption is granted when a company (not necessarily close) disposes of assets or an individual shares in a close company for the benefit of employees by way of a trust. In the latter case the trustees have to hold all or almost all the shares and effectively control the company. (S.149).

26 Chargeable Assets

No property so settled has to be applied for the benefit of a participator holding 5% or more of the shares, other than property taxable in the hands of the recipient.

If the transfer is not a gift, no gain or loss can arise, and the market value rules do not apply. The trustees acquire at the same price as the original owner if transferred at cost or less or in other cases at the actual price paid. For the small disposals rule an individual is deemed to have sold at the actual amount received, not at market value.

Private residences (Ss.101 to 105)

The general rule
An individual can gain whole or partial exemption from capital gains tax on the disposal of his main place of residence if certain conditions are fulfilled.

The main condition is that the residence must have been occupied throughout the period of ownership as the only or main residence, apart from the last two years of ownership.

The only or main residence
This includes any property occupied as such and can be a caravan provided it is set up and occupied as a residence, for example, a static caravan connected to the mains (MAKIN v. ELSON (1977) STC 46). A touring caravan temporarily occupied on a building site may not qualify (MOOR v. THOMPSON (1986) STC 176).

Grounds of up to one acre, including the site of the property, are also exempt. A larger area can be exempted provided it is required for the reasonable enjoyment of the residence. The Commissioners are the final arbiters of this should there be any dispute.

Other exemptions
Also exempted from charge are:

1. A property owned and intended for residence, except that the individual is living in job-related accommodation.

2. A house occupied rent free by dependant relative defined as a relative of the taxpayer or taxpayer's spouse who is incapacitated by old age or infirmity from maintaining him or herself, or a widowed, separated or divorced mother or mother-in-law. The size of income of the relative is irrelevant. A husband of wife only qualify for one such exempted property at a time.

3. A private residence owned by trustees and occupied as their main residence by a beneficiary or legatee, even if so occupied under a discretionary power (SANSOM v. PEAY, (1976) STC 494).

Chargeable Assets 27

Example

Brampton bought "Mon Repos" in April 1970 for £20,000 as the family's main residence. He then purchased "Don Romin" in April 1974 for £40,000 and elected "Mon Repos" as his main residence. "Mon Repos" was sold for £50,000 in April, 1982. From that date the family moved into "Don Romin" as the main residence and they sold it for £90,000 in April 1988.

The gain on "Mon Repos" is entirely exempt. The gain on "Don Romin" is assessed as follows:

Sale price		90,000
Cost	40,000	
Indexation (say)	20,000	(60,000)
Gross gain		30,000

Period of ownership (1974 to 1988): 14 years; period regarded as main residence: (on sale of "Mon Repos" — 1982 to 1988): 6 years.
Chargeable:

$$30,000 \times \frac{8}{14} \; (14-6) = 17,142$$

Ownership of more than one property

If an individual has two residences he may, within two years of acquiring the second, elect as to which one can be regarded as the main residence. If such as election is not made, the Inspector may subject to a right of appeal to the Commissioners, determine the matter. The two year time limit may be extended by the Revenue in certain circumstances.

A husband and wife living together can only have one exempted residence between them. Any transfer of a property from one to the other is deemed to be backdated to the acquisition of the transferor. If an interest in a property is transferred due to breakdown of marriage, the property can still be regarded as the main residence and thus exempt provided it continues to be occupied by the former spouse. This concession is lost however if the transferor acquires a further house as his main residence (ESC D5).

Periods of absence and others

Any period of ownership prior to 5th April, 1965 is not assessable for capital gains tax. The final two years of ownership is also exempt provided the property has been occupied at some time as the main residence. A period of up to one year before occupying the property is also exempt, provided the circumstances are reasonable, e.g. refurbishment, etc. (SP/D4).

Other periods of absence which are deemed to be exempt only apply if the period of absence comes in between earlier and later periods of occupation as the main residence, even if the property is let in the periods of absence. These are:
1. Any period or periods not exceeding three years in total.

28 Chargeable Assets

2. Any additional periods of any length when the owner was working wholly outside the UK.

3. Any additional periods up to a maximum of four years when occupation was prevented by the owner's employment, such as working and having to live elsewhere in the UK.

Example

Thompson purchases a property on 6th April, 1972 for 24,000 and sells it on 6th October, 1987 for 84,000.

6/4/72 to 5/10/72	The property was considerably renovated.
6/10/72 to 5/10/75	Thompson lived in the property as main residence.
6/10/75 to 5/4/80	Thompson lived away from home working elsewhere in the UK.
6/4/80 to 5/10/83	Thompson lived away from home working abroad.
6/10/83 to 5/10/84	Thompson lived in the property.
6/10/84 to 6/10/87	Thompson lived away from home.

Sale price		84,000
Cost	24,000	
Indexation	20,000	(44,000)
Gross gain		40,000

Chargeable:	Exempt:	
6/4/72 to 5/10/72 (½ year)	½	Renovation on ownership − less than 12 months
6/10/72 to 5/10/75 (3 years)	3	Living in property
6/10/75 to 5/4/80 (4½ years)	4	Working elsewhere in UK
	½	Up to 3 years for any reason
6/4/80 to 5/10/83 (3½ years)	3½	Working abroad (Any period exempt)
6/10/83 to 5/10/84 (1½ years)	1	Lived in property
6/10/84 to 6/10/87 (3 years)	2	Last two years of ownership

Total period of ownership 15½ years
Exempt　　　　　　　　14½ years
Taxable $40,000 \times \dfrac{1}{15\frac{1}{2}} = 2,800$

Business use and other occasions of charge

If part of the property has been used *exclusively* for trade or business, then that proportion of exclusive business use becomes chargeable. Note, only partial use for business which is not exclusive is not chargeable (e.g. use of spare bedroom as office and accommodating private guests).

Chargeable Assets   29

If, however, the now exempt proportion of a gain arises because the property has been wholly or partly let, the gain is only charged to the extent it exceeds, whichever of the following is the lower (5.80, FA, 1980):
1. £20,000; OR
2. the exempted gain on the part of the property occupied as the owner's residence.

Example
Mrs. Willis inherited the family home on the death of her husband in 1984, when the property was valued at £50,000. She let two thirds of it to students and lived in the remainder herself. She sold the property in 1988 for £90,000.

Sale price		90,000
Cost	50,000	
Indexation (say)	10,000	(60,000)
Gross gain		30,000
Exempted as own residence 30,000 × ⅓ =		10,000
Also exempted		
(own exemption or 20,000 whichever is lower)	10,000	(20,000)
Chargeable		10,000

Had the property been sold for £135,000 then the gain would be 135,000 − 60,000 = 75,000. The exemption would be:

Herself 75,000 × ⅓ =	25,000
Additional exemption (20,000 which is the lower of 25,000 and	20,000)
	45,000

Total gain	75,000
Total exemptions	(45,000)
Chargeable gain	30,000

The exemption does not apply if the let portion was self-contained accommodation, e.g. a separate flat with its own kitchen, bathroom and separate lockable entrance.

The exemption of the main residence does not apply if the property was acquired or expenditure incurred with a view to realising a gain on disposal.

Private residence exemption: separated couples
The Board of the Inland Revenue announced (on 22/10/73) that where as a result of the breakdown of a marriage one spouse ceases to occupy his or her matrimonial home and subsequently as part of a financial settlement disposes of the home, or an interest in it, to the other spouse (or, if the transfer is after a divorce, ex-spouse), the home may be regarded for the purposes of S.101 (exemption or relief from capital gains tax of an individual's main residence) as continuing to be a residence of the transferring spouse from the date his (or her) occupation ceases until the date of transfer, provided that it has throughout this period been the

30   **Chargeable Assets**

other spouse's only or main residence. Thus where a married couple separate and the husband leaves the matrimonial home while still owning it the usual capital gains tax exemption or relief for a taxpayer's only or main residence would be given on the subsequent transfer to the wife, provided she has continued to live in the house and the husband has not elected that some other house should be treated for capital gains tax purposes as his main residence for this period.

Debts

A debt is generally not a chargeable asset in the hands of the original creditor or his legatee.

However, this does not apply to holdings of any loan stock or similar security of any government, local or public authority, or any company. It is irrelevant that the loan stock is secured or unsecured. (S.134).

Options

"Option" includes double options, option payments, options to buy and sell and forfeited deposits and similar payments. (S.137).

The option is treated as a chargeable asset in the hands of the person granting it, but not in the hands of the person receiving it (this latter rule is to prevent the creation of a loss by abandoning the option, but see below for a relaxing of this rule in three special cases).

If the option is exercised, anything paid for it is incorporated with the price of the asset to form a single transaction for both parties.

Options are normally wasting assets and loss relief is thus restricted for losses incurred on the transfer of options relating to quoted shares which lapse or become valueless.

S.137 provides for relief on the abandonment of two types of option, contrary to the general rule. It applies when, on or after 20th April, 1971 there is an abandonment of either:

1. An option to subscribe for shares in a company which are quoted on a recognised stock exchange at the time of disposal.

2. A traded option to buy or sell shares in a company.

3. An option to acquire business assets which would otherwise have been used in a trade.

If an option is abandoned, then it is regarded as a disposal and the wasting asset rules are ignored. The abandonment of a trading option is also treated as a disposal.

Where an option is granted by a company whose shares are involved in a takeover i.e. where the consideration for a takeover bid is partly shares and partly an option to subscribe for shares, the option is regarded as equivalent to shares and therefore there is no chargeable occasion at that stage.

There are special rules for calculating the indexation allowance on the cost of an option to acquire an asset on the subsequent disposal of that asset. The cost of the option is treated as an item of expenditure separate from any cost incurred on the exercise of the option. The cost of the option is treated as incurred when the option was granted, and any cost on acquisition of the asset when the asset is acquired.

Traded options (quoted on a stock exchange) in company shares are not treated as a wasting asset, and the abandonment of such an option can thus give rise to an allowable loss. The option must be quoted on a stock exchange or the London International Financial Futures Exchange.

Commodity and financial futures and options

Gains arising from 6th April, 1985 onwards from dealings in commodity or financial futures or traded options which would usually be charged as income under Schedule D otherwise than as a trading profit (normally under Case VI) are now charged to capital gains tax or create allowable capital losses.

When a person closes out a futures contract, that transaction is looked on as the disposal of an asset consisting of the outstanding obligations of the contract, and any money or money's worth received or paid by him is treated as consideration for the disposal or as incidental costs of the disposal. When he does not close out a futures contract or as a result of its expiry date entitled to receive or liable to make a payment in full settlement of all obligations under that contract, he is treated as making a disposal of an asset consisting of those obligations, and the payment received or made is treated as consideration for or incidental costs of the disposal respectively.

"Commodity or financial futures" are those dealt in a recognised future exchange (e.g. London International Financial Futures Exchange (LIFFE) and other exchanges designated by the Board of Inland Revenue).

Chattels (S.128)

Introduction

"Chattels", as mentioned briefly earlier in the book, are the subject of special treatment in capital gains tax, classified as follows:

1. The treatment of chattels which are wasting assets, unless they are used in a business and capital allowances are claimable.

2. Chattels which are not wasting assets which are sold for less than £3,000 (£2,000 prior to 6, April, 1982).

3. Chattels which are part of a set.

The general conclusion is that the only chattels normally subject to capital gains tax are expensive collectors' items such as antiques, works of art, furniture and jewellery.

32 Chargeable Assets

A chattel is defined as "tangible, movable property", that is property with a physical presence (unlike a share or lease) and is movable, either by an individual or under its own power, such as a motor vehicle, aeroplane or ship.

Chattels which are wasting assets

A chattel which is also a wasting asset is exempted entirely from capital gains tax, unless it is used in a business and capital allowances are claimable.

"A wasting asset" is one with an estimated useful life of less than fifty years at the time of the disposal. Thus, if an object had an estimated life of say sixty years on acquisition and is sold twelve years later, it is exempted on the sale because at that time it only has a remaining useful life of forty-eight years which is less than fifty.

Chattels which are also wasting assets cannot be exempted if:

1. They have been used for the purposes of a trade, profession or vocation. AND

2. Capital allowances have or could have been claimed on the expenditure.

If these two conditions are satisfied, then a capital gain can be assessed on any gain made on sale and the claiming of capital allowances has no effect on the calculation of the gain which is simply the difference between sale price and original purchase price.

Example

A company buys a piece of machinery for £5,000 and claims 100% FYA on it. Two years later it sells the machine for £7,200.

On the sale the first £5,000 of the sale price would be deducted from the plant and machinery "pool" to calculate a balancing charge or reduce the written down value on which a WDA could be calculated. Such a sale price is restricted to historic cost.

The profit above historic cost (£2,200) is a chargeable capital gain.

There can never be an allowable capital loss on the sale of such a chattel because of the claim for capital allowances already having allowed the historic cost for tax purposes, and therefore to prevent a double tax allowance for any sale below historic cost (S.134).

There can still be relief from capital gains on a chattel on which capital allowances have been claimed if the asset is sold for less than £3,000.

If any asset is used only partly for business, the values, etc. are apportioned accordingly and the private proportion is exempted.

Assets owned on 6th April, 1965 are treated as if the capital allowances had been given on the notional value at 6th April, 1965 instead of original cost. A notional balancing charge is deemed to recover all gains up to the 6th April, 1965 value.

Chargeable Assets 33

Chattels which are not wasting assets disposed of for £3,000 or less
When durable chattels are disposed of for £3,000 or less gains are exempt and losses are not allowable. The disposal price is calculated gross, before the deduction of any expenses of sale. Thus, a picture sold for £3,100 with auctioneers', etc. expenses of £150 is not exempt if a gain is made.

If the disposal price is above £3,000 a form of marginal relief applies in that the assessable gain is limited to five thirds of the difference between the disposal and £3,000.

Example
Arty Tipe sells a painting for £3,300 having purchased it for £700. The expenses of sale were £200 and of purchase £50.

Gross gain:

Sale price		3,300
—Cost	700	
Expenses	250	
Indexation (say)	100	1,050
		2,250

Limited to assessable gain:

Sale price	3,300	
—Limit	3,000	
	300	$\times \frac{5}{3} = 500$

If an individual makes gains on other assets as well as a chattel, the tax payable is calculated using the marginal gain on the chattel.

Example
A man has, in the same tax year, gains on:

Shares			**Chattel**		
Sale price		7,400	Sale price		3,720
—Cost	900		—Cost	1,000	
Expenses	300		Expenses	200	
Indexation	100	(1,300)	Indexation	200	1,400
Gain		6,100	Gross gain		2,320
			Limited to:		
			$3,720-3,000=720\times\frac{5}{3}$	=	1,200
Total chargeable gains			7,300		

Tax payable:

$6,600\times$ Nil	=	Nil
$700\times30\%$	=	210.00
		210.00

34 Chargeable Assets

Losses can also be restricted. If both the disposal price and cost price are less than £3,000 then the loss is not allowed at all. If, however, the disposal price is less than £3,000 but the cost price (plus expenses) was over £3,000 the allowable loss is restricted by substituting a sale price of £3,000.

Example

A. Fool bought a painting for £3,500 and sold it for £1,600. The expenses of purchase were £100 and of sale £60.

Total loss:

Sale price		1,600
—Cost	3,500	
Expenses	160	
Indexation	300	(3,960)
		(2,360)

But this is limited to:

Sale price		3,000
—Cost	3,500	
Expenses	160	
Indexation	300	(3,960)
		(960)

Two or more articles which constitute a "set" are deemed to form a single asset if disposed of to the same or connected persons or persons acting in concert. A "set of articles" is not defined and must be decided in the circumstances of each individual case but presumably means articles connected to each other in terms of design, historically, etc. This provision is to prevent the sale of a set of articles in individual lots each for less than £3,000 and thus being exempt. In effect in considering the £3,000 limit the value of the whole set is what is relevant, not the sale price of the individual article. Apportionments are made as necessary.

Example

Connie Sir bought a set of six matching goblets for £1,000 in 1973.

Expenses of purchase £100. She sold:

1. Two of them for £1,050 to Joe Smith (expenses £60) on 6/6/86. The remaining four were then valued at £2,400.

2. The remaining four also to Joe Smith for £2,900 (expenses £110) on 9/11/87.

Chargeable Assets 35

Gain, 1986/87 (ignoring indexation):

Sale price				1,050
—Cost	1,000			
Expenses of purchase	100			

$$1,100 \times \frac{1,050}{1,050+2,400=3,450} = 335$$

Expenses of sale		60	395
	Gain		655

The assessable gain is limited to:
Deemed sale price

$$1,050+2,400=3,450$$
$$-3,000$$

$$450 \times \frac{5}{3} = 750 \times \frac{1,050}{1,050-2,400} = 228$$

Gain, 1987/88 (ignoring indexation):

Sale price			2,900
—Cost	1,000		
Expenses of purchase	100		
	1,100		
—Already allowed	335		
	765		
+Expenses of sale	110		875
			2,025

The assessable gain is limited to:

2,900+1,050 (sale price of part	3,950	
sold earlier)	−3,000	

$$950 \times \frac{5}{3} = 1,583$$
$$(-228 \text{ already} = 1,355$$
$$\text{allocated})$$

An apportionment is also necessary in appropriate circumstances to determine the size of allowable losses.

Example
Al Junk purchased four paintings constituting a set for £4,700 (expenses £200) in 1984. He sold them to Hiram J. Frankfurter IV, Junior as follows:

36 Chargeable Assets

1. Two of them for £800 (expenses £50) on 9/10/86. The value of the remaining two was estimated at £800.

2. The remaining two for £1,100 (expenses £80) on 17/6/83.

Loss, 1986/87 (ignoring indexation):

		Sale price			800
—Cost	4,700				
Expenses of purchase	200				
	4,900 ×	800		=	2,450
		800 + 800 = 1,600			
Expenses of sale				50	2,500
					(1,700)

Limited to:

$$3,000 \times \frac{800}{1,600} = 1,500$$

—Cost and expenses	2,500
	(1,000)

Loss, 1987/88 (ignoring indexation):

		Sale price		1,100
—Cost and expenses	4,900			
—Already allowed	2,450			
	2,450			
Expenses of sale	80			2,530
				(1,430)

Limited to:

3,000—1,500 (already allowed)	=	1,500
—Cost and expenses		2,530
		(1,030)

Reconciliation:

Total cost and expenses		4,900	
50+80	=	130	5,030
—Total sale price 800+1,100	=		1,900
			3,130

Limited to 5,030—3,000 = (2,030) given (1,000) 1986/87
(1,030) 1987/88

Certain gifts of works of art, etc. are exempt if given for the public benefit, etc. and the Treasury give a suitable direction.

Chargeable Assets 37

These provisions do not apply to commodities and to currency of any description. As Krugerrands are legal tender in South Africa they are not exempt from capital gains as chattels. Indeed, the Inland Revenue's view is that any profit made in dealing in them is a trading profit or assessable to Income tax under Sch.D, Case VI.

If a loss is incurred, the Inland Revenue attempt to treat it as a Sch.D, Case VI loss which can only be offset against other Sch.D, Case VI income.

Chapter Eight

Chargeable Occasions

When is there a chargeable occasion?

Capital gains tax applies to all gains accruing to a person on the disposal of chargeable assets. (S.1(1)).

As the legislation does not define "disposal" it has to be given its normal meaning, which therefore includes all sales, gifts and exchanges. The legislation does, however, extend the meaning of the word to include (S.19(1)):

1. Part disposals.
2. Where a capital sum is derived from an asset such as on receipt of compensation for damage, consideration for exploitation of an asset, and capital sums for the forfeiture or surrender of rights.
3. When an asset is lost or destroyed in spite of the fact that no money is received (S.22(1)).
4. When the value of an asset has been reduced to a negligible figure (S.22(2)).
5. On certain occasions during the life of a trust.

When some of the occasions mentioned above apply, special rules are used to compute the gain, and these are examined later in this book.

Some occasions are specifically exempted from being chargeable disposals, these being:

1. On the transfer of an asset from one spouse to another.
2. All gifts to charities and certain bodies concerned with preserving the national heritage.
3. The transfer of an asset as security for a mortgage or loan.
4. Companies in inter-group transfers.
5. Death.

Time of acquisition and disposal

Where an asset is disposed of by one person and acquired by another under a contract, the time at which the disposal and acquisition is made is the time the contract is made, and not (if different) the date of conveyance of the asset (S.27).

There are certain modifications to the general rule in special circumstances:

1. Where a disposal arises from a compensation payment, then disposal takes place when the compensation is received.

Chargeable Occasions 39

2. If a contract is conditional, the relevant time is when the contract is satisfied, especially if an option is granted then it is the date the option is fulfilled.

3. When compulsory purchase of land takes place, the relevant time is generally when the compensation is agreed or otherwise determined by arbitration. However, if the authority enters on the land under its powers before the agreement of compensation, the date of entry becomes the relevant time. (S.111).

Gifts

General
When a person makes a gift of a chargeable asset there is a disposal for capital gains tax purposes, (TURNER v. FOLLET (1973) STC 148), the property being deemed to have been disposed of at its market value. However, there can be rollover relief on a gift from individual to individual, or trustees. A gain on a business asset can be rolled over when gifted to a company.

Gifts in settlement
The same rules apply generally as to gifts. However, if on the occasion of a gift in settlement the donor or the spouse retains an interest in the settlement, no loss can be allowed on the occasion of the gift (*Para. 4, Sch. 7, ICTA* 70).

Exemptions on gifts to charities, etc. (S.146)
As from 21st March, 1972 when a disposal is made to a charity or one of the bodies concerned with the National heritage and listed in paragraph 12, Sch. 6, Finance Act, 1975 (national museums, the National Trust, etc.), and it is otherwise than under a bargain at arm's length, then the following provisions apply.

Disposals by way of gift are exempted, including gifts in settlement and sales for a consideration not exceeding the expenditure allowable. The disposal and acquisition are deemed to be made for a price which ensures no gain and no loss.

On a disposal by charity or other body, the donor's acquisition is treated as being that of the body making the disposal.

The exemption also applies to certain deemed disposals when a charity, etc. becomes entitled to assets, or they are held for a charity, etc.

1. On the occasion of a charity, etc. becoming absolutely entitled to settled property.

OR

2. On the termination of a life interest, but not including a termination by the death of the entitled person.

Death

On a death after 30th March, 1971 assets of which the deceased was competent to dispose of are deemed to be acquired by his personal representatives (or anyone else on whom they devolve) at their market value at the date of death, but there is no disposal for capital gains (S.49).

40 Chargeable Occasions

When the assets are disposed of by the personal representatives to the legatees there is again no disposal for capital gains. When the legatee acquires the asset he is deemed to have acquired it (for CGT purposes) at the date of death and at its value on death.

Example
Bibby died on 12/2/76. His only asset was:
A block of shares in the family company purchased in 1967 for £30,000. On 19/2/76 they were worth £62,000.
They were left entirely to his son who sold them for £90,000 on 16/5/87. The son's capital gain would be (for 1987/88):

	Sale price		90,000
—	Acquisition value	62,000	
	Indexation (say)	8,000	70,000
	Assessable gain		20,000

If the personal representatives dispose of an asset other than to a legatee, there is a chargeable disposal but they qualify for the same reliefs as an individual in the year of death and the two following years.

Example
Brown died on 11/8/85. He left an estate valued at £180,000 and to obtain ready cash the executors sold the following assets:
1. On 2/2/86, shares in ABC Ltd. for £10,000 (valued at £7,200 on death).
2. On 19/8/87, shares in DEF Ltd. for £19,000 (valued at £12,000 on death).
3. On 5/5/88, shares in GHI Ltd. for £9,000 (valued at £4,000 on death).

Assessments:

1985/86	$10,000 - 7,200 = 2,800 \times$ Nil	
	(below annual exemption) =	Nil
1986/87	No disposals.	
1987/88	$19,000 - 12,000 = 7,000.$ $6,600 \times$ Nil =	Nil
	$400 \times 30\% =$	120.00
		120.00
1988/89	$9,000 - 4,000 = 5,000 \times 30\% =$	1,500.00

If the personal representatives make losses they cannot be passed back against the previous gains of the deceased, but if the deceased himself had incurred losses himself in the fiscal year up to when death occurred, they can be carried back against the gains of the three previous years of assessment, taking a later year before an earlier one (S.49(2)) The losses need only be utilized to the extent they reduce the net gains to the exempt level for the appropriate fiscal year.

Chargeable Occasions 41

Example

White died on 20/7/87 having made chargeable gains of £2,000 and losses of £6,300 in 1987/88. He had gains of £6,700 in 1986/87, £5,100 in 1985/86 and £5,000 in 1984/85.

Assessments:

	Gains	**Loss**	**Tax payable**	
		(6,300)		
1987/88	2,000			Nil
	(2,000)	2,000		
	Nil	(4,300)		
1986/87	6,700			Nil
	(1,700)	1,700		
	5,000	(2,600)		
1985/86	5,100			Nil
	(2,100)	2,100		
	3,000	(500)		
1984/85	5,000		$5,600 \times$ Nil =	Nil
	(500)	500	$900 \times 30\%$ =	270.00
	4,500	Nil		270.00

Revision questions

1. Cooper purchased a house in April, 1955, for £4,000 plus expenses of purchase of £200. He lived in it up to April, 1968, and then let it. He finally sold it in April, 1985, for £27,000 with expenses of sale of £800. The value of the house on 6th April, 1965, was £5,200. What was the assessable gain on the sale? Ignore indexation.

2. Smith purchased a house in September, 1964, for £3,000 plus expenses of purchase of £150. He occupied it as his residence until April, 1967, and then moved away to work elsewhere in the UK at his employer's insistence. He was away until April, 1973, and then moved back to the house. He moved out again in September, 1974, and sold it in April, 1987, for £25,000 with sale expenses of £700. Calculate the assessable gain on sale. Ignore valuation at 6th April, 1965. Also ignore indexation.

3. Which of the following are assessable:

(a) A V.C. medal sold by Bloggs at Sothebys. It was won by his great grandfather in the Crimean war.

(b) Jones surrenders a life assurance policy on his own life and gets £2,000.

(c) Green buys War Loan on 1/7/86 and sells at a profit on 1/9/87.

(d) A Ming vase purchased for £6,000 and sold for £9,000.

(e) A yacht purchased for £25,000 and sold for £40,000.

Ignore indexation in calculating the gains.

42 Chargeable Occasions

(f) Bellows purchased a painting for £2,000 in 1984 and sold it for £4,200 in 1987.

(g) Grocott purchased a painting for £4,000 in 1984 and sold it for £2,200 in 1987.

Ignore indexation in all cases.

Answers

1. Sale price	27,000−800=	26,200
Less: Purchase price	4,000+200=	(4,200)
	Total gain	22,000

Gain arising after 6/4/65 (time apportionment):
22,000×20/30= 14,667

Valuation at 6/4/65:

Sale price		26,200
Less:		(5,200)
	Gain	21,000

Assessable gain after exemption for certain periods:
Total period after 6/4/65=20 years
Assessable, April, 1968 to April, 1985= 17 years less last 2 years = 15 years.
Assessable gain $14,667 \times {}^{15}\!/_{20} = 11,000$.

2. Sale price	25,000−700=	24,300
Less. Purchase price	3,000+150=	3,150
	Total gain	21,150

Gain arising after 6/4/65:

Total period of ownership Sept. 1964 to April, 1987.	22½yrs.
Total period after 6/4/65	22 yrs.

$21,150 \times {}^{22}\!/_{22\frac{1}{2}} = 20,680$.

Assessable gain:

Occupied April, 1965 to April, 1967	=	2
Exempted (working elsewhere) April, 1967 to April, 1971	=	4
(3 years exemption) April, 1971 to April, 1973	=	2
Occupied April, 1973 to September, 1974	=	1½
Last 2 years	=	2
Total exempted		11½

Assessable period   10½ years (22−11½)
Gain:
    20,680×10½/22=9,870

3. (a) Exempted, ownership came from direct inheritance.

(b) Exempted.

(c) Exempted.

(d) Chargeable. A Ming vase being an antique has an anticipated life of more than fifty years and is not therefore a wasting asset. The gain is £3,000 (ignoring indexation).

(e) Exempted, as it is a chattel which is also a wasting asset.

(f)

Sale price	4,200
Cost	(2,000)
Gross gain	2,200

But limited to $4,200 - 3,000 = 1,200 \times \frac{5}{3} = 2,000$.

(g)

Sale price	2,200
Cost	(4,000)
Less	1,800

But allowable loss limited to $4,000 - 3,000 = (1,000)$.

Chapter Nine

Rules of Computation

The normal calculation

Introduction

The normal calculation is a very simple one. From the total sale price is deducted (Ss.32 and 33).

1. The capital cost of acquisition. If the asset was created then the costs of creation.

2. Capital additions or improvement since acquisition (but not repairs or maintenance).

3. The incidental costs of purchase and sale. These can include:

(a) Selling agent's commission.

(b) Professional valuation fees.

(c) Legal costs.

Note that the incidental costs of disposal are not generally deducted from the sale price separately. This can be important e.g. when deciding if a chattel is sold for more or less than £2,000 (see the list of exemptions).

4. Every deductible expense is then increased in proportion to rises in the Retail Price Index from the date the expenditure was incurred to the date of disposal (the indexation allowance).

Some types of expenditure are specifically disallowed:

1. Costs of repair and maintenance.

2. Costs of insurance.

3. Anything which ranks as a deduction for income tax purposes.

4. Any expenditure or part of it which is recouped from public funds.

Example

Partridge purchased a property in 1975:

Cost	16,500	
Legal costs	300	
During his ownership he expended money on:		
Repairs and maintenance		1,207
Cost of enlarging and improving the premises (in June, 1982)		2,796

Rules of Computation 45

He sold the property in August, 1986:

Sale price	52,600		
Valuation fees	420		
Estate agents' fees	789		
Legal costs	700		

The taxable gain is:

Gross sale price			52,600
Less:			
Capital cost	16,500		
Incidental costs	300		
	16,800		
Indexation allowance (say)	3,400	20,200	
Costs of capital improvement	2,796		
Indexation allowance (say)	380	3,176	
Incidental costs of sale	420		
	789		
	700	1,909	25,285
Assessable gain			27,315

Assets not sold for cash or full value

When an asset is not sold for full value or is part of an exchange deal, the market value of the asset is used as the deemed sale price for the vendor and the deemed cost for the purchaser — both parties must use the same figure. The market value is used (S.19(3))

(Note—if an asset is disposed of but not acquired by someone else e.g. it is destroyed, the disposal value is treated as nil):

1. When an asset is not sold commercially e.g. a gift.

2. When an asset cannot be valued e.g. when given for personal services rendered or is acquired on the loss of a job.

3. When an asset is acquired on a notional disposal (death, bankruptcy, etc.) or in settlement of a debt.

4. When an asset is disposed of to a "connected person" (Ss.25 and 62).

"Market value" is defined as "the price which those assets might reasonably be expected to fetch on sale in the open market". Both transferor and transferee have to adopt the same value, and no consideration is to be taken of any reduced price which might result from a bulk sale.

The market value will apply unless the transferor and transferee jointly elect for it not to apply. An election must be made within two years of the end of the appropriate year of assessment. Thus, UK residents acquiring assets as a gift from a non-resident are now deemed to acquire it at market value (S.66, FA, 1984).

46 Rules of Computation

"Connected persons" are defined as members of the same family, persons connected with the same trust, business partners and persons connected through a company (S.63). Appendix 1 gives a full definition and deals with other restrictions placed on transactions between connected persons.

Example
Joe Parsonby acquired a painting for £3,000 in 1975 and gave it to the trustees of his family settlement in May, 1986 when it was valued at £5,600. The trustees sold it at Christeby's for £7,800 in August 1987. Joe does not make a gifts rollover election.

Gain of Joe Parsonby, 1986/87:

Deemed sale price		5,600
—Cost	3,000	
Indexation allowance (say)	300	(3,300)
Assessable gain		2,300

Gain of the trustees, 1987/88:

Sale price		7,800
—Deemed cost	5,600	
Indexation allowance (say)	100	(5,700)
Assessable gain		2,100

Note: Gifts can, of course, be the subject of an election to rollover the deemed gain from the transferor against the deemed cost of the transferee.

Exclusion of value which is assessable elsewhere

Generally receipts assessed to income tax (or corporation tax) are not also assessed to capital gains and therefore do not suffer a double charge to tax. Examples are the sale of patent rights, lump sums received by an employee on retirement (S.31). However, there is no such disallowance of a double charge when capital transfer tax is involved on a lifetime gift. Then, the same asset can suffer both CTT and CGT.

There are also certain disposals which are relevant both for income tax (or corporation tax) and capital gains tax. However, unlike capital transfer tax, the same value is not assessed twice, there is a compensating adjustment. Examples are:

1. Premiums on short leases assessable under Schedule A (dealt with later).

2. Disposals of items which have been the subject of capital allowances (dealt with later).

3. If a person receives something in exchange for the disposal of an income bearing source, the capitalised value of that income bearing source can be brought into charge for capital gains tax, as well as the income assessed to income tax.

Indexation allowance

Introduction

In calculating the taxable gain on any disposal from April, 1982 onwards, an addition has been made to the capital expenditure to allow for the effects of inflation as measured by the Retail Price Index. However, the original regulations contained two main restrictions:

1. The calculation of the indexation allowance excluded any inflationary increases for the first twelve months of ownership.

2. The indexation allowance could not be used to create or increase a loss.

For disposals from 6th April, 1985 (1st April, 1985 for companies) both these restrictions have been swept away and indexation now applies from the month expenditure is incurred to the month of disposal.

However the new rules did not come into force until 28th February, 1986 for disposals of loan stock or similar securities to which the anti-bond washing provisions apply.

Indexation is also applied to any disposal where there is no gain/no loss situation, so that the person acquiring the asset takes it over at the original cost of the disposer plus any indexation allowance.

Calculation of indexation allowance

The indexation allowance is calculated by comparing the Retail Price Index for the month expenditure is incurred either on acquisition or improvement with the Index for the month of disposal. The resultant percentage increase is rounded to three decimal places. See Appendix 3 for comments on the retail price index.

Expenditure on acquisition is regarded as incurred in the month when the asset is acquired. Expenditure on improvements is deemed to be incurred when it is due and payable, even though it may not increase the value of the asset until later.

Example

White acquired a property in August, 1985 for 50,000 incurring incidental costs of 1,000. He spent 10,000 improving it in June, 1986 and sold it for 108,000 in October, 1988 incurring incidental costs of 1,800.

Assume RPI figures of:

August, 1985	95.49
June, 1986	97.79
October, 1988 (say)	130.00

Sale price				108,000
Cost			51,000	
Indexation allowance:				
$51,000 \times \dfrac{130 - 95.49}{95.49}$		$(0.361) =$	18,411	69,411
Improvements			10,000	

48 Rules of Computation

Indexation allowance:

$$10,000 \times \frac{130-97.79}{97.79} \quad (0.330) = \quad \underline{3,300} \quad 13,300$$

Incidental costs		$\underline{1,800}$ $\underline{84,511}$
Gain		$\underline{23,489}$

A claim may be made for the indexation allowance due on an asset held on 31st March, 1982 to be calculated by reference to its market value on that date rather than its cost. A claim must be made within two years of the end of the year of assessment or accounting period of disposal, but this period can be extended at the Inland Revenue's discretion. The effect of such a claim is also taken into account where an apportionment of costs is necessary under the rules relating to assets derived from other assets (S.36, CGTA, 1979).

Example

A company purchases a building in June, 1980 for 240,000 incurring incidental costs of 2,800. Its value at 31st March, 1982 is 310,000. The building is sold for 450,000 in June, 1987, the incidental costs being 3,500. The company makes an election for indexation to be applied on the asset's value at 31st March, 1982.

    Assume RPI figures of:

March, 1982	79.44
June, 1986 (say)	110.00

Sale price		450,000
Cost	242,800	

Indexation allowance:

$$310,000 \times \frac{110-79.44}{79.44} \quad (0.385) = \quad 119,350 \quad 362,150$$

Incidental costs		$\underline{3,500}$ $\underline{(365,650)}$
Gain		$\underline{84,350}$

Unlike the systems operative before April, 1985, indexation can now apply to losses, increasing an actual capital loss or can be used to create one.

Example

A company purchases a building in May, 1983 for 100,000 with incidental costs of 1,500. The building is sold in September, 1986 for:

1. 200,000.
2. 110,000.
3.   94,000.

Indexation adds 20,000 to the original cost and incidental expenses.

Sale price		200,000	110,000	94,000
Cost	101,500			
Index allowance	20,000	121,500	121,500	121,500
	Gain	78,500	Loss (11,500)	(27,500)

Disposals subject to "no gain/no loss" results

Many transactions are specifically ruled not to give rise to a chargeable gain or allowable loss e.g. transfers from husband to wife, transfers between companies in the same group, gifts relief elections, etc. If appropriate (i.e. the relevant transfer took place after April, 1985) the recipient of an asset on such an occasion can elect for indexation to be applied to 31st March, 1982 value on any subsequent disposal.

Example

Boris acquired a building in 1980 for £10,000. He gifted it to Sidney in July, 1983 when it was worth £40,000. Sidney sold it in August, 1986 for £110,000. Its value at 31st March, 1982 was £30,000.

RPI:

March, 1982	79.44
July, 1983	85.30
August, 1986	97.82

Original computation:

Transfer price from Boris to Sidney:

Original cost	10,000
Indexation $10,000 \times \dfrac{85.30 - 79.44}{79.44} =$	740
(0.074)	10,740

On sale by Sidney he could elect to substitute for that acquisition value of 10,740 with indexation from July, 1983:

Acquisition value	10,740
Indexation (July, 1983 to August, 1986)	
$10,740 \times \dfrac{97.82 - 85.30}{85.30} =$	1,579
(0.147)	12,319

50 Rules of Computation

The following could be substituted by Sidney making the appropriate election:

Original value of Boris	10,000
Indexation (March, 1982 to August, 1986)	

$$30{,}000 \text{ (Value at March, 1982)} \times \frac{97.82 - 79.44}{79.44} = \quad 6{,}930$$

(0.231)	16,930

Thus the gain chargeable on Sidney's disposal would be:

Sale price	110,000
Deemed acquisition value	16,930
Chargeable gain	93,070

Special rules of computation

General

There are three occasions when special rules are adopted. These special rules always follow the same general principles, but are adapted to specific circumstances as needed. They occur again and again throughout capital gains tax and the reader would be well advised to become familiar with them to understand the subject thoroughly, and watch out for them when later chapters deal with specific assets.

They are:
1. Part disposals.
2. The postponement of liability by applying "rollover" relief.
3. Assets owned on 6th April, 1965.

Part disposals (S.35)

When only part of an asset is sold, there is still a chargeable occasion, e.g. the sale of part of a building or the creation of a lease out of a freehold interest (S.19(2)).

The gain is calculated generally by use of the "part disposal formula" which only deducts(from the sale price) part of the cost of the whole. The formula is:

$$\text{Cost of the whole asset} \times \frac{\text{Amount received on part disposal (i.e. sale price)}}{\text{Amount received for part disposal (i.e. sale price again)} + \text{Market value of part retained}}$$

Example

A building was purchased for £30,000 in April 1983 and part of it sold for £45,000 in May, 1984 when the value of the part retained was £75,000. RPI: April 1983: 84.28; May 1987 (say) 105.00.

Rules of Computation 51

Sale price			45,000
$-30,000 \times \dfrac{45,000}{45,000+75,000}$	=	11,250	
Indexation			
$11,250 \times \dfrac{105-84.28}{84.28}$	(0.246) = 2,768		(14,018)
Gain			30,982

There are four subsidiary rules:

1. Only expenditure common to the whole asset is apportioned. Any expenditure wholly attributable to the part sold or retained is dealt with as appropriate.

Example

A building is purchased for £14,000 with £600 legal costs in 1976. Part is sold in August, 1978 for £10,000 with £750 of legal costs applying to the sale. The value of the remainder (in August, 1978) is £18,000. The part retained is later improved in April 1984 at a cost of £3,000 and sold for £37,000 with legal costs of £850 in July, 1987.

Gain on part disposal in 1978/79:

Sale price		10,000	
$-14,600 \times \dfrac{10,000}{10,000+18,000}$	=5,215		
Legal costs		750	
			(5,965)
Assessable gain			4,035

Gain on disposal of remainder in 1987/88:

Sale price				37,000
Remaining cost 14,600—5,215=		9,385		
Indexed (from March 1982)	(say)	2,000	11,385	
Improvements		3,000		
Indexed (from April 1984)	(say)	500	3,500	
Legal costs			850	(15,735)
Gain				21,265

2. If an asset (of which a part if sold) qualifies for capital allowances then the part disposal rules are applied first and any adjustments for capital allowances are made later (to the part sold).

3. Special rules apply to the disposal of subleases and are dealt with later.

4. On a part disposal the deductible expenditure has to be apportioned, and the indexation allowance calculated only on the apportioned expenditure to be deducted.

52 **Rules of Computation**

The "rollover" principle

When a chargeable asset is technically disposed of and immediately (or within a short period) is replaced with another asset of a similar kind, the liability can be postponed until the replacement is disposed of generally by reducing the actual cost of the replacement by the chargeable gain on the original, and thus arriving at a "deemed" cost for capital gains tax purposes.

Examples of when this rollover principle is used are:

1. Transfer of a business from an individual to a company (Chapter 18).

2. Company mergers and takeovers when shares of one company are exchanged for those of another (Chapter 15).

3. The replacement of one business asset by another (Chapter 19).

4. When compensation is received for damage or destruction to an asset and is used to repair it (Chapter 13).

5. Gifts of assets from one individual to another (Chapter 11).

6. Gifts of business assets by individuals (Chapter 20).

All have special rules applying and are dealt with in detail elsewhere in the book, but the basic principle can be seen in all of them. (See Chapters 11, 19 and 20 for more detailed treatments).

Example

A company purchased factory A in 1985 for £100,000 and sells it in 1987 for £140,000 replacing it with factory B at a cost of £185,000. B is later sold for £210,0000 and not replaced.

Gain on A:

Sale price		140,000	
—Cost	100,000		
Indexed	10,000	(110,000)	
Gain		30,000	—not assessed but rolled over against cost of B

Gain on B:

Sale price			210,000
—Actual cost of B	185,000		
Rolled over gain on A	30,000		
		155,000	
Indexed (on 155,000)		14,000	
Deemed cost of B			(169,000)
Assessable gain on sale of B			41,000

The £41,000 gain could again be rolled over if B was replaced with C.

Rules of Computation 53

Assets held on 6th April, 1965

When an asset was owned at 6th April, 1965 (when capital gains tax was first introduced) the aim is to tax only the part of the gain which has accrued from then to the date of disposal. There are alternative ways of doing this:

1. Calculate the total gain (sale price minus cost) and arithmetically apportion the gain from 6th April, 1965 to date of sale. When this is done, assets purchased before 6th April, 1945 are deemed to have been purchased on that date. This is known as the "time apportionment formula" (para. 11, Sch. 5). See Appendix 2 where additional expenditure was also incurred prior to 6th April, 1965.

2. Take the gain calculated by deducting the value of the asset at 6th April, 1965 from the sale price. This method has to be elected for by the taxpayer, and is not automatically applied by the Inland Revenue, except when land with development value is concerned, when 6th April, 1965 value is the only method which can be used (para. 12, Sch.5).

These two methods are the alternatives which can be applied to all assets apart from land with development value (mentioned above) and quoted shares (which are dealt with later).

Example

Fred Green acquired a painting for £1,200 on 6th April, 1940 and sold it for £25,000 on 6th October, 1985. It was worth £8,000 on 6th April, 1965. Indexation is ignored.

Cost with time apportion- ment method			6th April, 1965 method	
Sale price	25,000		Sale price	25,000
—Cost	$\underline{1,200}$	$20\frac{1}{2}*$	—Value at 6/4/65	8,000
	$23,800 \times \frac{20\frac{1}{2}*}{40\frac{1}{2}**}$			
=	12,047			17,000

Obviously the taxpayer would not elect for valuation at 6/4/65.

Notes: *20½ years is the period from 6/4/65 to 6/10/85 (the chargeable period). **40½ years is the period from 6/4/45 (purchase date earlier than then) to 6/10/85.

The time limit for making an election for 6th April, 1965 value is two years from the end of the year of assessment in which the disposal takes place (Para. 12, Sch.5).

One snag about deciding whether or not to make this irrevocable election especially in connection with unquoted shares where there is no readily identifiable market value at 6th April, 1965, is that the Inland Revenue will not enter into negotiations as to the amount of the market value until the irrevocable election has been made — taxpayers and their agents should therefore be very certain of the value of assets at 6th April, 1965 before making this election.

54 Rules of Computation

For disposals on or after 6, April, 1982 (1, April, 1982 for companies) both the original cost (before applying time- apportionment) and 6, April, 1965 value have both to be index- linked from a base month of March, 1982.

Example

A man purchased a property for £20,000 on 6, April, 1960. Its value at 6, April, 1965 was £24,000. He sold it on 6, April, 1987 for £46,000. Value in March 1982: £30,000.

Assume RPI:

March, 1982		79.64
April, 1987	(say)	104.00

Sale	price		46,000
Cost		20,000	
Indexation allowance	$30,000 \times \dfrac{104-79.44}{79.44}$ =	9,270	
	(0.309)		(29,270)
			$16,730 \times {}^{22}/_{27} =$
			13,631

Sale price				46,000
6, April, 1965 value			24,000	
Indexation allowance	$30,000 \times$	0.309	=	9,270 33,270
				12,730

There are two restrictions on the use of the 6th April, 1965 valuation, both concerned with the allowance of capital losses:

1. If the 6th April, 1965 valuation produces a loss greater than a loss calculated by reference to original cost, only the lower loss is allowable.

Example

A man bought an asset on 6th April, 1960 for £9,091 and sold it on 6th April, 1986 for £8,000. Its value on 6th April, 1965 was £10,909.

Original cost			**6th April, 1965 value**		
Sale price		8,000	Sale price		8,000
—Cost	9,091		—Value	10,909	
Indexation	909	(10,000)	Indexation	1,091	(12,000)
Loss		$(2,000) \times {}^{21}/_{26}$	Loss		(4,000)
	=	(1,616)			

As the election would substitute a larger loss than the loss for the whole period of ownership, only the smaller loss is allowable. If, however, the loss by reference to 6th April, 1965 is less than the overall loss calculated by reference to cost, but more than the time- apportionment loss, the 6th April, 1965 calculation is allowed to stand.

Rules of Computation 55

Example

A man bought an asset on 6th April, 1962 for £6,364 and sold it on 6th April, 1986 for £5,400. Its value on 6th April, 1965 was £6,273.

Original cost			**6th April, 1965 value**		
Sale price		5,400	Sale price		5,400
—Cost	6,364		—Value	6,273	
Indexation	636	(7,000)	Indexation	627	(6,900)
Loss		(1,600) $\times 2\frac{1}{24}$	Loss		(1,500)
		= (1,400)			

The allowable loss is £1,500. Whilst it is greater than the time- apportionment loss it is less than the OVERALL loss, and this is what matters.

2. If there is a loss by reference to market value at 6th April, 1965 and a gain by reference to original cost, the result is treated as if there were neither gain nor loss.

Example

A man bought an asset for £5,455 on 6th April, 1963 and sold it for £9,000 on 6th April, 1986. Its value on 6th April, 1965 was £8,727.

Original cost			**6th April, 1965 value**		
Sale price		9,000	Sale price		9,000
—Cost	5,455		—Value	8,727	
Indexation	545	6,000	Indexation	873	9,600
Cost		3,000 $\times 2\frac{1}{23}$	Loss		(600)
		= 2,739			

There is therefore no assessable gain or allowable loss.

Obviously, if a 6th April, 1965 value substituted a gain for loss over the whole period of ownership, the taxpayer would not make the election, and the original loss would stand.

Example

A man bought an asset for £7,273 on 6th April, 1962 and sold it for £6,500 on 6th April, 1986. Its value on 6th April, 1965 was £5,364.

Original cost			**6th April, 1965 value**		
Sale price		6,500	Sale price		6,500
—Cost	7,273		—Value	5,364	
Indexation	727	8,000	Indexation	536	5,900
Loss		(1,500) $\times 2\frac{1}{24}$	Gain		600
		= (1,312)			

The taxpayer would not make the election and therefore there would be an allowable loss of £1,312.

56 **Rules of Computation**

Appendix I

Connected persons

The aim of this legislation is to prevent avoidance of CGT by arrangements between persons who have connections which are not wholly commercial.

The general rule is that when an asset is passed between such persons the transaction is treated as not being at arms length, and the asset is valued on disposal at market value. (S.19(3)).

If a loss results, it can only be relieved against gains arising on transactions with the same person. (S.62).

There are rules to counteract the artificial results which may be obtained by the use of options and restrictive covenants between connected persons.

The definition of a connected person is: (*Para.21, Sch.7*)

1. Family, spouse, and direct relatives of self or spouse (ancestors, lineal descendants, brothers and sisters).

2. Trustees. A trustee or a settlement of which the individual is a settlor, with any person connected with such an individual, and with any body corporate connected with the settlement.

3. Partnerships. Members are connected with each other or with the relative of any partner.

4. Companies. Companies are connected with any person who is a member of a controlling group, and with other companies which are under the same control.

Assets transferred to close companies

Special rules apply when a person transfers assets to a close company over which he or a connected person has control.

A person controlling such a company for years before 6/4/65 could avoid CGT by transferring an asset to the company and selling the shares for an enhanced value, but only paying tax on the gain theoretically arising from 6/4/65.

In such a case the shares of the company are deemed to be acquired at the date the asset was transferred. (Para. 16, Sch.5).

This rules applies where a person (or a connected person) has control (or a substantial holding of shares) of a close company and the straightline apportionment (para. 11, Sch.5) applies to the caclulation of the gain on those shares after the transfer for the asset.

The paragraph does not apply where a loss is made on the shares.

Rules of Computation 57

Assets disposed of in a series of transactions (S.71, FA 1985)
When a person disposes of assets to another person or persons with whom he is connected by way of two or more "material transactions which are linked, and the "original market value" of the assets disposed of in the transactions is less than the portion of the "aggregate market value" then the value used in calculating the gain is the appropriate portion of the aggregate market value.

These rules are not to apply to disposals between husband and wife.

A "material transaction" is one which takes place on or after 20th March, 1985 and two or more such transactions are linked if they occur within a period of six years ending on the date of the last transaction.

These rules are activated, when a second material transaction brings a series of linked transactions into being and also an existing series of transactions is extended by including one more (whether or not an earlier transaction ceases to be part of the series).

When a series of transactions spans 20th March, 1985, any transactions which occurred before that date but not more than two years before the first transaction occurring on or after that date, are treated as within the new provisions.

Example
Euriah Muggins gives shares in his family company, Burnham Extinguishers Ltd. He originally held 60 shares out of 100 issued. Shares in a majority holding are worth £500 each, those in a minority holding £100 each. He purchased them for £1 each. He sells 8 shares to his son, Constantius in May, 1986 for £100 each.

He then sells 20 shares to his son in July, 1987 for £100 each.

He then sells another 25 shares to Constantius for £100 each in September, 1988.

The gains would have been:

$$1986/87 \quad 800 - 8 = 792$$
$$1987/88 \quad 2{,}000 - 20 = 1{,}980$$
$$1988/89 \quad 2{,}500 - 25 = 2{,}475$$

These can be revised to the value appropriate to a majority holding value on Constantius acquiring overall control from his father in under 6 years:

$$1986/87 \quad 8 \times 500 = 4{,}000 - 8 = 3{,}992$$
$$1987/88 \quad 20 \times 500 = 10{,}000 - 20 = 9{,}980$$
$$1988/89 \quad 25 \times 500 = 12{,}500 - 25 = 12{,}475$$

Transactions between group companies which are deemed to be no gain/no loss, are not material transactions. However, if a company acquires an asset from another group member on or after 20th March, 1985 and then disposes of it by way of a material transaction to a person connected with a second company which had disposed of it (on or after 20th March, 1985) by way of an inter-group transfer, then the two inter-group transfers were the same, or between the two there was no other disposal, then in trying to determine if these provisions apply, the disposal by the first company is deemed to have been made by the second company, but any deemed increase in the value of the assets is applied to the first company.

58   **Rules of Computation**

Appendix 2

Time-apportionment formula where more than one item of expenditure prior to 6th April, 1965

When additional capital expenditure has been incurred in addition to the original cost, the same formula applies. As a first step, the total gain is apportioned in accordance with the separate parcels of expenditure (i.e. original cost and subsequent additional capital expenditure). Each part of the total gain is then apportioned in accordance with the formula to find that part falling after 6th April, 1965.

The complete formula is:

$$E(0) \frac{T}{P + T} \quad E(1) \frac{T}{P(1) + T} \quad E(2) \frac{T}{P(2) + T}$$

WHERE:

E(0) is the part of the total gain apportioned to the original expenditure. E(1) and E(2) are the parts of the gain apportioned to any subsequent additions.

P, P(1) and P(2) are the respective periods before 6th April, 1965. Capital expenditure is deemed to take place on the date the contract was signed or, if there is no contract, on the date the work was begun.

When an asset is acquired without cost, such as goodwill, the period of apportionment begins to run from the date of its creation or 6th April, 1945, whichever is later. If there has been capital expenditure after the date of creation, the gain attributable to that expenditure is estimated separately, and the balance attributed to the period commencing at the beginning of the period of ownership.

Example

A taxpayer purchased an asset on 6th April, 1935 for £7,000. There was additional expenditure on 6th April, 1952 of £4,000. There was additional expenditure on 6th April, 1958 of £3,000. The asset was sold on 6th April, 1987 for £24,000. The value at the 6th April, 1965 is ignored.

The gain is as follows:

1. The total gain is:

		£
Sale price		24,000
Less: 7,000+4,000+3,000 =	14,000	
Indexation (say)	6,000	(20,000)
		4,000

Rules of Computation 59

2. The gain is apportioned:

$$E(0) \quad \frac{4{,}000 \times 7{,}000}{14{,}000} \qquad = \qquad 2{,}000$$

$$E(1) \quad \frac{4{,}000 \times 4{,}000}{14{,}000} \qquad = \qquad 1{,}143$$

$$E(2) \quad \frac{4{,}000 \times 3{,}000}{14{,}000} \qquad = \qquad 857$$

$$\overline{4{,}000}$$

3. The chargeable gain for each part is calculated per the time- apportionment formula:

$$E(0) \quad 2{,}000 \times \frac{22}{20+22} \qquad = \qquad 1{,}047$$

$$E(1) \quad 1{,}143 \times \frac{22}{13+22} \qquad = \qquad 718$$

$$E(2) \quad 857 \times \frac{22}{7+22} \qquad = \qquad 650$$

$$\text{Total chargeable gain} \qquad \overline{2{,}415}$$

If there has been a part disposal before 6th April, 1965, the date of the part disposal and the market value of what then remains is taken as being the acquisition date and the acquisition price of the remainder. This latter is generally calculated by an arithmetical apportionment (Para. 11, Sch.5).

Appendix 3: Retail price index

Gains arising on the disposal of an asset may be reduced by an indexation allowance. The allowance is calculated by reference to increases in the index after March 1982.

The index was recalculated from January 1987 when under the old system it was 394.5 (January 1974, 100). In January 1987 the recalculation began with a base figure of 100, and therefore the figures given below are not those given at the time by the Department of Employment.

Readers should be aware, therefore, that calculations prior to January 1987 may use figures from the previous index.

	1982	1983	1984	1985	1986	1987
January	–	82.61	86.84	91.20	96.25	100.0
February	–	82.97	87.20	91.94	96.60	100.4
March	79.44	83.12	87.48	92.80	96.73	100.6
April	81.04	84.28	88.64	94.78	97.67	
May	81.62	84.64	88.97	95.21	97.85	
June	81.85	84.84	89.20	95.41	97.79	

60 **Rules of Computation**

July	81.88	85.30	89.10	95.23	97.52
August	81.90	85.68	89.94	95.49	97.82
September	81.85	86.06	90.11	95.44	98.30
October	82.26	86.36	90.67	95.59	98.45
November	82.66	86.67	90.95	95.92	99.29
December	82.51	86.89	90.87	96.05	99.62

Revision questions

Work out the capital gains on the following.

1.   A man purchases an investment property in May 1979, for 20,000 (including expenses). He spends 25,000 on extending it and improving it in August 1983. He sells part of the premises for 30,000 in August 1987 when the portion retained was valued at 50,000. The expenses of sale were 1,400. The value of the property in March, 1982 was 40,000.

2.   A man purchases an investment property in May 1979 for 30,000 (including expenses). In August 1983 he spent 40,000 on improving the entire building. In March, 1986 he spent 10,000 on improving one portion of it. This same portion was sold for 60,000 in August 1987 when the part retained was valued at 80,000. The costs of sale were 1500. The value of the premises in March 1982 was 68,000.

3.   A man purchased a building for 40,000 in April, 1960. It was valued at 46,000 on 6th April, 1965. Its value on 31st March, 1982 was 70,000. It was sold for 180,000 in April 1987, the costs of sale being 3,000.

4.   A man purchased a building for 70,000 in April 1960. It was valued at 80,000 in April 1965 and at 140,000 in March 1982. It was considerably extended at a cost of 50,000 in August 1983 and sold for 300,000 in April 1987, expenses of sale being 3,000.

RPI:

March 1982:	79.44
August 1983:	85.68
March 1986:	96.73
April 1987: (say)	105.00
August 1987: (say)	110.00

Answers

1. Sale price   30,000

Cost $20{,}000 \times \dfrac{30{,}000}{30{,}000+50{,}000=80{,}000}$ =   7,500

Index (at March 1982 value):

$40{,}000 \times \dfrac{30{,}000}{80{,}000} = 15{,}000$

$\times \dfrac{110-79.44}{79.44}$ (0.385)   =   5,775   13,275

Improvements $25{,}000 \times \dfrac{30{,}000}{80{,}000}$ =   9,375

Index (from August, 1983):

$9{,}375 \times \dfrac{110-85.68}{85.68}$ (0.284) =   2,663   12,038

Expenses of sale   1,400   (26,713)

Gain   3,287

2. Sale price   60,000

Cost $30{,}000 \times \dfrac{60{,}000}{60{,}000+80{,}000=140{,}000}$ =   12,857

Index (at March, 1982 value):

$68{,}000 \times \dfrac{60{,}000}{140{,}000} = 29{,}142$

$\times 0.385$ (*see answer 1*)   =   11,220   24,077

Improvements to whole: $40{,}000 \times 60{,}000 = \dfrac{}{140{,}000}$ 17,143

Index (from August, 1983):

$17{,}143 \times 0.284$ (*see Answer 1*)   =   4,869   22,012

Improvements to part sold: 10,000

Index (from March, 1986):

$10{,}000 \times \dfrac{110-96.73}{96.73}$ (0.137)   =   1,370   11,370

Expenses of sale   1,500   (58,959)

Gain   1,041

62 Rules of Computation

3. Gain based on cost:

Sale price			180,000
Cost		40,000	

Index (based on March 1982 value):

$$70,000 \times \frac{105 - 79.44}{79.44} \ (0.322) = 22,540 \qquad 62,540$$

Costs of sale		3,000	(65,540)

$$114,460 \times \frac{22^*}{27}$$
$$= 93,263$$

*22 years = April 1965 to April 1987.
27 years = April 1960 to April 1987.

Gain based on 6th April 1965 value:

Sale price		180,000
Value in April 1965	46,000	
Index (based on March 1982 value)		
See above −	22,540	
	68,540	
Expenses of sale	3,000	(71,540)
		108,460

The assessable gain would be based on original cost, 92,263.

4.

Sale price				300,000
Cost			70,000	
Index (from March, 1982)				
140,000 × 0.385 (*see Answer 1*)	=		53,900	123,900
Extension			50,000	
Index (from August 1983)				
50,000 × 0.284 (*see Answer 1*)	=		14,200	64,200
Costs of sale				3,000 (191,100)
Gross gain				108,900

Apportion gain:

Cost	70,000	
Extension	50,000	
Total	120,000	

$$\text{Original purchase} \qquad 108,900 \times \frac{70,000}{120,000} = 63,525$$

$$\text{Extension} \qquad 108,900 \times \frac{50,000}{120,000} = 45,375$$

$$108,900$$

Rules of Computation 63

Time apportion gain based on original cost:

$63,525 \times \dfrac{22}{27}$ (see Answer 3) =   51,761

Based on 6th April, 1965 value:

Sale price			300,000
6/4/65 value	80,000		
Index (from March, 1982)	53,900	133,900	
	50,000		
Extension plus indexation	14,200	64,200	
Costs of sale		3,000	(201,100)
			98,900

Apportion gain:

Purchase (based on April 1965 value)	80,000
Extension	50,000
Total	130,000

Purchase $98,900 \times \dfrac{80,000}{130,000}$ =   60,681

Extension = same as above   =   45,375

Chargeable gain:

Purchased (based on cost with time-apportionment)	51,761
Extension	45,375
Total	97,136

Chapter Ten

General Relief for Gifts (S.79, FA, 1980)

General

When (from 6th April, 1980 onwards) an individual disposes of a chargeable asset at a consideration less than full market value to another individual or trustees of a settlement resident in the United Kingdom, they can make an election (joint election in the case of individual giving to individual but only the donor makes the election in the case of a gift to trustees) to apply rollover relief to the gain which would otherwise be assessable on the disposer by reference to the asset's market value.

The recipient takes a cost price for capital gains equivalent to the actual purchase price paid (not the full market value) or the disposer's cost price in the case of a gift, suitably amended for indexation.

Example

Joe Bowler purchased, in 1975, 1,000 shares in the National Wicket Co. Ltd. for £7,000. He sold them to his friend George Duckham in 1980 for £11,000 when their true market value was £24,000. (No capital transfer tax was payable). George Duckham sold them for £40,000 in 1987.

Joe Bowler – 1980/81:

Actual sale price	11,000	Market Value	24,000
−Cost	7,000	Cost	(7,000)
Gain assessable	4,000		17,000
			(4,000)
		Rolled over gain	13,000

George Duckham – 1987/88:

Sale price		40,000
Market value on acquisition	24,000	
−Rolled over gain	13,000	
Deemed cost	11,000	
Indexation allowance (say)	4,000	(15,000)
Gain assessable		25,000

The relief is available on the making of a joint election if the transferor and transferee are individuals. Only the transferor need make the election if the transferee is a body of trustees.

The transferee has to be resident and ordinarily resident in the UK at the time of transfer and must remain so for the six years after the year of transfer if he has not disposed of it in the meantime.

If the transferee ceases to be resident or ordinarily resident in the UK in this period a gain of the rolled over amount is deemed to accrue to him before he leaves (S.79, FA, 1981). This procedure does not apply if:

1. The reason for his leaving the U.K. is to take up employment abroad; and

2. He again becomes resident and ordinarily resident in the U.K. within three years from when he ceases to be so resident and ordinarily resident.

If the tax is not paid within twelve months of its payable date, the transferor can be assessed. The transferor then has a right of recovery against the transferee as from 6, April, 1982. The gifts relief is also available to trustees on their transferring assets at less than full market value (S.82, FA, 1982).

Capital transfer tax (inheritance tax)

If capital transfer tax or inheritance tax is payable on the transaction, then the recipient of the asset can increase his base cost by the amount of the capital transfer tax paid, no matter how it was calculated or who paid it. The addition of capital transfer tax or inheritance tax to the base cost cannot however create an allowable loss.

Example
Al Eagle purchased in 1976 1,000 shares in Shady Enterprises Ltd. For £16,000. In 1981 he gifted them to his niece, Connie Stable, when they were worth £50,000. They jointly made an election to roll over the gain. Al paid the CTT as donor, it costing him £7,000. Connie sold the shares for £68,000 in 1987.

Al Eagle − 1981/82:

Market value	50,000	
Cost	(16,000)	
Deemed gain	34,000	
Cost to Connie 50,000−34,000=		16,000

Connie Stable − 1987/88:

Sale price		68,000
Acquisition value (after rollover)	16,000	
CTT paid on acquisition	7,000	
	23,000	
Indexation allowance (say)	8,000	(31,000)
Gain assessable		37,000

66 Receipts of Interest

If the inheritance tax is subsequently adjusted (after the original payment) then suitable alterations are made to the capital gains tax charged by raising a further assessment, or by way of a discharge or repayment. An example would be the death of the transferor within seven years of making the gift.

Example
Say, in the example above, Al Eagle died of lead poisoning (by too close proximity to a violin case) in 1987, and Connie had to pay a further £4,000 IHT, then:

Original gain	37,000
Additional IHT*	(4,000)
Readjusted gain	33,000

A repayment of $4,000 \times 30\% = 1,200$ would be made.

Note: *No indexation allowance as the additional IHT is only payable after the disposal.

Indexation allowance

An indexation allowance must be applied, if the usual conditions are satisfied, to cost on the making of a gift, and only the reduced gain rolled over.

On any subsequent disposal by the transferee, an indexation allowance can be made again.

Any capital transfer tax or inheritance tax paid on the original transfer and added to the transferee's cost is also index linked on any subsequent disposal, unless it only becomes payable on a subsequent death within seven years of the date of the gift.

Example
Birley acquired a property for £22,000 in June, 1981. He gave it to his married daughter, Mrs. Morton on August, 1982 when it was worth £30,000 and Birley paid CTT of £3,000 in April, 1983. Mrs Morton sold the property for £50,000 in January, 1987.

RPI:		
	June, 1982	81.85
	August, 1982	81.90
	April, 1983	84.28
	August, 1983	85.68
	January, 1986	100.00

Birley's disposal, August, 1982:

Market value			30,000
Cost		22,000	
Indexation allowance $22,000 \times \dfrac{81.90 - 81.85}{81.85}$ (0.001)			22 (22,022)
Gain			7,978

Mrs. Morton's disposal, January, 1987:

Sale price				50,000
Acquisition value		22,022		
Indexation allowance $22,022 \times \dfrac{100-81.90}{81.90}$ (0.221) =		4,867	26,889	
CTT paid (April, 1983)		3,000		
Indexation allowance $3,000 \times \dfrac{100-84.28}{84.28}$ (0.187) =		561	3,561	(30,450)
Gain				19,550

Effect of retirement relief

If retirement relief is available on the disposal, this reduces the gain which can be rolled over.

Example

Ruby Demoutta, aged 66, after a long and successful career as managing director and controlling shareholder of the Metropolitan Mobsters Co. Ltd., gifts his shares to his niece Lottie Talerna in 1980. He originally bought his shares for £102,000, and they are worth £260,000 on the occasion of the gift. Lottie pays CTT of £60,000 on the transfer and sells the shares to Mr. Dapappa for £300,000 in 1987. Ruby qualified for full retirement relief in 1985.

Mr. Demoutta — 1980/81:

Market value	260,000
− Cost	(102,000)
Gross gain	158,000
Retirement relief	(50,000)*
Rolled over gain	108,000

*(Maximum of retirement relief in 1980)

Mrs. Talerna — 1987/88:

Sale price			300,000
Value on acquisition	260,000		
Rollover	108,000		
Deemed acquisition value	152,000		
Indexation allowance (say)	38,000	190,000	
CTT paid	60,000		
Indexation allowance (say)	15,000	75,000	(265,000)
Gain			35,000

Gain covered by retirement relief.

Chapter Eleven

Losses

General

Losses are computed the same as gains. If apportionment is necessary (e.g. with an acquisition before 6th April, 1965) this is applied as for a gain. (S.29).

A loss is not allowable to a person not resident or ordinarily resident in the year the loss is made.

Losses must be allowed against the gains of the year they accrue. If not, they are carried forward without time limit but must be set off as soon as possible. Losses cannot be carried back, neither can they be set against income assessable to income tax (or against other types of profit assessable to corporation tax for companies).

The losses of husbands and wives have already been dealt with.

Loss or destruction of an asset where no capital sum is received (S.22(1) & (3)) The loss or destruction of an asset is a chargeable occasion, and therefore a loss can accrue. There is no disposal however, (and therefore no loss), when an option is abandoned.

When a building is destroyed, the whole asset is not strictly destroyed, as the definition of a building includes the land it stands on and this remains. However, for this purpose only, the building can be regarded as a separate asset and the owner can be given loss relief on its destruction.

The land is treated as if, on the destruction of the building, the site had been sold and reacquired on that date. Thus any increase in the value of the land over cost may partly or completely offset the loss on the building, but when the land is sold at some future date the chargeable gain will be resultantly smaller.

Example
A building was purchased for £60,000 in November, 1972 the site costing an additional £10,000.

The building is uninsured and is destroyed by fire in May, 1986. The value of the site at the time of destruction is £20,000. The site is subsequently sold in August, 1988 for £40,000.

The allowable losses and assessable gains are:

		£
Cost of building		60,000
Value of site on destruction (with indexation)	24,000	
Less: Site cost (with indexation)	12,000	12,000
Allowable loss, 1986/87		(48,000)
Sale of site		40,000
Less: Deemed cost	24,000	
Indexation	3,000	27,000
Chargeable gain, 1988/89		13,000

13,000—The loss of (£48,000) can be offset against this if it has not previously been used.

When the value of an asset has become negligible (S.22(2))

When an assets value has become negligible the owner can apply to the Revenue to treat it as though he had sold and reacquired it at the current market value, thus establishing a useable loss.

Any subsequent sale might give rise to a gain, calculated by reference to the new acquisition price.

In strictness the sale and reacquisition is deemed to occur when the claim is made, but in practice the Revenue are prepared to accept that the sale and reacquisition take place on a particular date. The time limit for making such a claim is now two years from the end of the year in which that date takes place (Inland Revenue statement of 4/8/75).

Losses on loans and guarantees to traders (S.136).

Irrecoverable losses are allowed on:
1. Loans to traders.
2. Payments by a guarantor.

When the loan or guarantee was given on or after 12th April, 1978. Loans must qualify by:
1. Not being a debt on a security.
2. The borrower must use it wholly for the purposes of or the setting up of a trade by him, and the trade must not consist of or include money lending.
3. The borrower must be resident in the UK.

70 Losses

The lender must claim the loss and satisfy the Inspector the money is irrecoverable, or that the payment under the guarantee has been made, and the claimant has not assigned his rights.

The relief is not available:

1. Between spouses living together.

2. Between companies in the same group.

3. When the loan has become irrecoverable in consequence of the terms of the loan or any arrangement of which the loan forms part.

4. Because of any act or omission of the lender or guarantor.

The loss is allowed to the lender at the date of his claim and to a guarantor when he makes his payment.

Indexation allowance

Up to 5th April, 1985 (31st March, 1985 for companies) an indexation allowance could not create or increase a loss.

However, as from 6th April, 1985 (1st April, 1985 for companies), these rules have been altered so that an indexation allowance is now calculated irrespective of whether it reduces a gain, converts a gain to a loss, or increases a loss.

Example
Allen Ltd. purchased a property for 50,000 in April, 1983. They sold it in July, 1987 for:

1. 40,000.

2. 52,000.

3. 80,000.

Indexation adds 10% to the basic cost, increasing it to:

Cost	50,000
Indexation allowance (10%)	5,000
Allowable cost	55,000

Sale price:

	40,000		52,000		80,000
Allowable cost	55,000		55,000		55,000
Allowable loss	(15,000)	Allowable loss	(3,000)	Taxable gain	25,000

Chapter Twelve

Assets Restored or Replaced (S.21)

There is a disposal every time money is derived from an asset, whether or not it has been sold. Such occasions are the receipt of capital sums by way of compensation or insurance for damage or loss of an asset. When this happens, a capital gain probably results. (S.20(1)).
1. Sums derived from assets not lost or destroyed.
2. Those derived from assets lost or destroyed.

Assets not lost or destroyed

On the receipt of money there is no assessment to capital gains tax if:
1. The cash is used wholly to restore the asset.
OR
2. Is used for restoration except a small amount not required for that purpose. If the unused money is less than 5% of the total received, it is not assessed and is treated as being ''small''
OR
3. The total amount received is small in comparison with the value of the asset. Again, less than 5% is treated as being small.

The receipt, if not assessed, is treated as reducing the cost of the asset, and increases the amount of any gain on a subsequent disposal — yet another form of rollover relief.

Example

An asset costing £4,000 suffers fire damage for which £2,000 is received by way of insurance. The value of the asset is £5,000 at the time of the fire. The amount spent on repairs is:
- (a) £2,000
- (b) £1,910

(a) No gain assessable, no adjustment of original cost.

(b) The amount not spent is less than 5% of the amount received, so for future disposals the cost is adjusted:

Original cost	£4,000
Less: Amount unspent	90
Adjusted	£3,910

72 Assets Restored or Replaced (S.21)

Also the cost would have been adjusted if the total amount received was less than £250 (5% of value at the time of the fire).

If the amount not spent is greater than 5%, then the taxpayer has two alternatives:

1. To have the whole of the receipt treated as a disposal and assessed to tax, by not claiming relief.

OR

2. To have that part of the capital sum used in restoration not included in the disposal receipt, but deducted from the allowable cost of the next disposal. The remainder of the compensation received is then assessed as a part disposal. The amount spent on replacements can then be added to the remaining cost, and effectively wipes out the deduction referred to above.

Example

An asset was purchased for £3,000, partly destroyed for which £4,000 was received. Only £2,200 was spent on renovations. It was worth £5,000 after renovation. The taxpayer could claim:

1. To have the whole £4,000 treated as a receipt on a disposal.

OR

2. Have £1,800 treated as a receipt on a part disposal and the amount actually spent deducted from the cost carried forward:

			£
Received			1,800
Less: $3{,}000 \times \dfrac{1{,}800}{1{,}800 + 5{,}000}$	=	794	
Indexation allowance (say)		60	(854)
Assessable gain			946
Carry forward remaining asset at an unallowed cost of:			
Original cost			3,000
Less: Used in part-disposal		794	
Spent in renovations		2,200	2,994
			6
Plus: Additional allowable expenditure			2,200
Carry forward			2,206

Assets lost or destroyed

If an asset is totally lost or destroyed, any amount received can be exempted from tax so long as it is used to buy a replacement within twelve months of receipt, or any longer period the Revenue will allow.

The cost of the new asset is reduced by the theoretical gain on the old asset plus any scrap value of the old asset.

Example

An asset costing £4,000 is totally destroyed. Insurance proceeds are £4,500 and the scrap value is £200. The replacement costs £6,000:

	£		
Cost of new asset			6,000
Gain on old asset: Receipts		4,500	
Cost	4,000		
Indexation allowance (say)	150	4,150	350
Scrap value		200	550
Deemed cost			5,450

If not all the receipt is spent on a replacement, no claim such as above can be made. However, if the amount unspent is less than the gain, then the assessed gain is restricted to the amount unspent and the balance is deducted from the cost of the replacement.

Example

An asset costing £6,000 is totally destroyed. £7,000 is recovered in insurance, but only £6,600 is spent on a replacement.

Say to the gain is:

Receipts		7,000
Cost	6,000	
Indexation allowance (say)	150	6,150
Gain		850

The amount unspent, £400, being lower than the actual gain (£850), is assessed. The replacement cost of £6,600 is reduced by £450 (remainder of the gain) to £6,150 for any future capital gains computation.

Revision questions

1. A taxpayer bought a shop on 1st July, 1948, for £4,000 with expenses of purchase of £200. He extended the property on 30th September, 1960, at a cost of £1,000. The property was sold on 31st March, 1987, for £20,000 with expenses of sale of £500. The value of the property at 6th April, 1965, was £7,000. Ignore indexation.

2. A building was destroyed by fire in October, 1980, there being no insurance. It had been purchased in May, 1976, for £10,000 in total the site being valued at that time for £2,000. The undeveloped site was sold in February, 1988, for £10,000. At the time of the fire the site was valued at £2,400. Ignore indexation.

74 Assets Restored or Replaced (S.21)

Answers

1.

Sale price 20,000—500		=	19,500
Less: Purchase price 4,000+200+1,000		=	5,200
	Total gain		14,300

The gain is apportioned:

$$14,300 \times \frac{4,200}{5,200} = 11,550$$

$$14.300 \times \frac{1,000}{5,200} = 2,750$$

Time-apportionment:

$$11,550 \times \frac{22}{38\frac{3}{4}} = 6,557$$

$$2,750 \times \frac{22}{26\frac{1}{2}} = 2,283$$

Assessable gain	8,840

Gain on valuation at 6/4/65:

Sale Price		19,500
Less: 6/4/65 valuation		7,000
	Gain	12,500

2.

Cost 10,000—2,000		8,000
Less: Value of site on date of fire	2,400	
Site cost	2,000	400
	Allowable loss	7,600
Sale of site		10,000
Less: Deemed cost		2,400
	Assessable gain, 1987/88	7,600

Chapter Thirteen

Value Shifting
(S.26)

This is a measure to prevent the avoidance of capital gains whereby value is transferred by a series of transactions from one asset to another, the final increase in value being arranged to be non-taxable.

A disposal is caught if it has been arranged that the value of the asset disposed of is materially reduced and that either:

1. The person making the disposal.
2. A person connected with him.

OR

3. Any other person (unless he was not connected with the others and it can be shown tax avoidance was incidental to the operation), has received a tax-free benefit.

The arrangements concerned need not have been made before the disposal, to cover the circumstance in which an asset is disposed of before its acquisition. The tax free benefit need not be received as a result of the disposal.

Chapter Fourteen

Stocks and Shares

Introduction

In practice and in examination papers, marketable securities are probably the most important form of asset. The rules described in this Part of the book apply generally to (S.65).

1. Shares quoted on a recognised stock exchange.
2. Unquoted shares.
3. Company securities, such as debentures.
4. Commodity futures and currency.

The relevant situations for capital gains tax purposes that are studied in this part are:

1. The general rules of valuation and computation of gains and losses.
2. Capital distributions.
3. The making of a scrip or rights issue.
4. Some other form of reorganisation of the share capital.
5. The takeover of one company by another, with a resultant exchange of shares in one company with those in another, and also, probably, a transfer of assets from one company to another.
6. Shares were acquired prior to 6, April, 1965.
7. Special miscellaneous rules (not dealt with) apply to:

(a) Shares held as a result of a person's employment, and there is a restriction on the right of resale.

(b) Where a bonus issue is made instead of a cash dividend.

Special rules (some of them already outlined) apply to:

1. Government securities. These have already been dealt with.
2. Approved unit and investment trusts.
3. Compensation stock.
4. Shares and securities acquired within a prescribed period of time (see Appendix 1).

Stocks and Shares 77

Valuation and general rules of computation

When shares are sold the disposal value is generally the sale price, but as with other assets there are occasions when a market value has to be computed e.g. gifts, death, etc.

Some special anti-avoidance rules applying to the disposal of shares and securities within a prescribed period of acquisition are examined in the Appendix.

Quoted securities (S.150(3))

The market value is determined from figures given in the Stock Exchange official daily list for the relevant day in one of two ways, and the lower value is used:

1. The "quarter up" rule. To the lower of the mean average of prices for the day is added one quarter of the difference between the low and high mean averages. These figures are normally quoted as the closing prices.

2. The "half up" rule. The half way price between the actual lowest and highest bargains struck on the day. This figure is always used for valuing shares on 6, April, 1965. The "quarter up" rule is not available as an alternative for that day.

Example

Hamish McHamish gives his trustees 7,000 £1 ordinary shares in Aberdeen Granite Rock Cakes Ltd. on 17, November, 1988. The relevant figures on that day were:

1. Closing prices (per share) 100p and 108p.
2. Bargains struck 96p (lowest) 116p (highest).

The values for capital gains purposes are:

"Quarter up" rule $\qquad$ $100 + 2 \quad (\frac{1}{4} \times 108 - 100) \quad = \quad 102p$

"Half up" rule $\qquad$ $96 + 10 \quad (\frac{1}{2} \times 116 - 96) \quad = \quad 106p$

The disposal value would therefore be (using the "quarter up" rule):

$$7,000 \times 102 = £7,140.00$$

Similar rules are, of course, used for inheritance tax.

Valuation of unquoted shares

As there is no established market like the Stock Exchange for the sale of unquoted shares, their valuation (when there is no sale in an arm's length transaction) is a complicated and very specialized topic. The Inland Revenue have a special division, the Shares Valuation Division, which deals with it both for capital gains and for capital transfer tax purposes.

Often both capital transfer tax and capital gains tax are payable on the same gift of shares. The same value does not necessarily apply on the same gift for both taxes as each has its own special rules of valuation. However, the same value is taken for both purposes on death. Even though at death capital gains is not payable, the shares need to be revalued to calculate the recipient's deemed cost.

The valuation of unquoted shares is too specialized and too complicated a topic to be dealt with in this book, but some of the special rules of valuation for capital gains tax are examined in Appendix 2.

78 Stocks and Shares

Appeals or questions on the valuation of unquoted shares arising on or after 13, April, 1975 are dealt with only by the Special Commissioners.

General rules of computation

The rules of identification of matching sales of shares of the same class in the same company with previous purchases, if more than one, have changed frequently in recent years:

1. Up to the introduction of indexation (5th April, 1982 for individuals 31st March 1982 for companies), sales were in general, matched with purchases on a "first in, first out" (FIFO) basis, but purchases on or after 6th April, 1965 were "pooled", that is separate purchases were not matched with particular sales, but an average price used.

Example
Noah had these transactions in Ark Construction Enterprises, plc:

Transaction:	Date:	No. of shares		Price (£)	
Bought	March, 1964	1,000		3,000	
Value	6th April, 1965	1		4 per share	
Bought	June, 1976	400		2,000	
Bought	April, 1978	600	1,000	5,000	7,000
Sold	October, 1980	1,700		20,400	

Calculation of gain (using FIFO):
Sale of 1,000 shares (purchased March, 1964) = Sale price:
$$20,400 \times \frac{1,000}{1,700} = 12,000$$

Cost	3,000	
6/4/65 value 1,000×4 =	4,000	4,000
Gain		8,000

Sale of 700 shares (from post-April, 1965 pool):
$$20,400 \times \frac{700}{1,700} = 8,400$$

Cost $7,000 \times \dfrac{700}{1,000}$ $= 4,900$

Gain   3,500

Total gain 8,000+3,500 =   11,500
"Pool" to carryforward

Shares	Price (£)
1,000−700 = 300	7,000−4,900 = 2,100

(For a more detailed treatment of computations involving pre-April, 1965 purchases, see later).

Stocks and Shares 79

2. With the introduction of indexation as from April, 1982 the rules were changed to give effect to the twelve month rule before indexation was applied to cost. Sales were then matched with purchases on a "last in first out" (LIFO) basis. Sales were matched with purchases in this order:

a) Purchases in the previous twelve months (and therefore indexation did not apply to cost). Within that twelve months, the earliest purchases were deemed sold first.

b) Purchases more than twelve months old and on or after 6th April, 1982 (1st April, 1982 for companies).

c) A pool of shares involving all purchases between 6th April, 1965 and 5th April, 1982 (31st March, 1982 for companies). Purchases and sales in 1981/82 involved special transitional rules — called "1982 holdings or 1982 pool".

d) Pre-April, 1965 purchases.

Example

Samson has the following transactions in the £1 ordinary shares of Temple Demolitions plc:

Transaction	Date	No. of shares	Price (£)
Bought	February, 1983	400	1,200
Value	6th April, 1965	1	2 per share
Bought	April, 1967	300	1,500
Bought	October, 1970	500	4,000
Bought	May, 1982	200	2,000
Bought	December, 1983	600	8,000
Sold	April, 1984	1,800	19,800

Calculation of gain (using LIFO):   **Total**

Sale of 600 shares (purchased December, 1983):

Sale price $19,800 \times \dfrac{600}{1,800} =$ 6,600

Cost (no indexation)   8,000

Loss   (1,400)

Sale of 200 shares (purchased May, 1982):

Sale price $19,800 \times \dfrac{200}{1,800} =$ 2,200

Cost   2,000

Indexation (say)   100   2,100

Gain   100

80 Stocks and Shares

Sale of 700 shares (1982 pool):

Sale price $19,800 \times \dfrac{700}{1,800} =$ 7,700

Cost $4,000+2,000$ $=$	6,000	
Indexation (say)	600	6,600
Gain		1,100

Sale of 200 shares (purchased February, 1963):

Sale price $19,800 \times \dfrac{200}{1,800} =$ 2,200

Cost $\qquad 1,200 \times \dfrac{200}{400} =$ 600

Value 6/4/65 $200 \times 2 =$	400	
Cost	600	
Indexation (say)	60	660
Gain		1,540
Total gain		1,340

Carry forward from February, 1963 purchase 200 shares at an original cost of 600 (400 6/4/65 value). (For a more detailed treatment of pre-April, 1965 purchases, see later).

3. For all disposals from 6th April, 1985 (1st April, 1985 for companies) the rules have altered again with:

a) The abolition of the twelve month rule for indexation.

b) The right to elect for indexation at 31st March, 1982 value if the shares were acquired before then.

In the original 1985 Finance Bill there was also a proposal to revert back to a FIFO (first in, first out) method of identification of sales with purchases, but this was altered in the later Parliamentary stages, and therefore the LIFO (last in, first out) method still applies.

Example

Moses has the following dealings in the £1 ordinary shares of Tablets (Stone Masons) plc:

Transaction	Date	No. of shares	Price (£1)
Bought	June, 1978	1,200	4,000
Bought	April, 1981	600	3,000
		1,800	7,000
Value	31st March, 1982	Per share	£4 each
Bought	October, 1985	800	6,800
Sold	December, 1987	2,000	20,000

Retail Price Index:

March, 1982	79.44
October, 1985	95.59
December, 1987 (say)	105.00

Calculation of gain (using LIFO):   **Total**

Sale price (October, 1985 purchase) $20,000 \times \dfrac{800}{2,000} = 8,000$

Cost   6,800

Indexation $6,800 \times \dfrac{105 - 95.59}{95.59} = $ 667   (7,467)   533

(0.098)

Sale price (1982 pool) $20,000 \times \dfrac{1,200}{2,000} = $ 12,000

Cost $7,000 \times \dfrac{1,200}{1,800} = $ 4,667

Indexation:

$1,200 \times 4 = 4,800$ (March, 1982 value)*

$\times \dfrac{105 - 79.44}{79.44} = $ 1,546   (6,213)   5,787

(0.322)

Total gain   6,320

*Note: Do not forget acquisitions prior to April, 1982 can be indexed at March, 1982 value.

When qualifying expenditure is increased because of the cost of acquiring an option, there is an additional increase to the indexed pool of expenditure. The increase is an amount equal to the indexed rise in the option consideration between the month in which the option is exercised and the later of the month in which the option was acquired or March, 1982.

Bed and breakfasting

When securities which would affect the same pool are purchased and sold within a ten day period, they are matched, and only the excess, if any, increases or decreases the pool. There is no indexation allowance when securities, etc. are disposed of within ten days of purchase.

82 Stocks and Shares

Example
Peter has the following transactions in the shares of Inland Seas Fisheries plc:

Transaction:	Date	No. of shares	Price (£)
Bought	17/5/87	600	3,500
Bought	29/7/88	400	5,000
Sold	7/8/88	300	6,800

R.P.I. (estimated):

May, 1987		103.00
July, 1988		120.00
August, 1988		122.00

Sale 8/8/88:

Sale price (300 shares)	6,800
Cost (29/7/88) $5,000 \times \dfrac{300}{400} =$	3,750
(No indexation)	2,150

May, 1987 purchase:

	Shares		Price
	600		3,500
Indexed rise (to July, 1988)		$3,500 \times \dfrac{120-103}{103} \ (0.165) =$	578
			4,078
Bought 29/7/88	400		5,000
	−300	100	−3,750 1,250
		700	5,328

Transactions from April 1985

In calculating the gain or loss on a disposal of shares, using last in, first out (LIFO) the following pools are created.

a) All purchases of the same share since 6th April, 1982 (1st April, 1982 for companies) are pooled in what is called the "new pool". Every time there is an acquisition or disposal the pool is revised and updated for indexation:

Stocks and Shares 83

Example

Parker has the following dealings in the £1 ordinary shares of Smith Enterprises plc:

Disposals after 6th April 1985

	Date	**No. of shares**	**Price**
Purchase	9th March, 1983	900	3,400
Purchase	11th November, 1984	600	3,000
Sale	4th July, 1985	200	6,000
Purchase	27th October, 1985	400	7,000
Sale	1st March, 1987	500	9,000

R.P.I.:

March, 1983	82.12
November, 1984	90.95
July, 1985	95.23
October, 1985	95.59
March, 1987 (say)	103.00

Sale, 4/7/85:

Sale price (200 shares)   6,000

	Shares		**Price**
9/3/83	900		3,400

Index to November 1984:

$$3,400 \times \frac{90.95 - 83.12}{83.12} = 320$$
$$(0.094)$$

           3,720

11/11/84 purchase	600	3,000
	1,500	6,720

Index to July 1985:

$$6,720 \times \frac{95.23 - 90.95}{90.95} = 316$$
$$(0.047)$$

           7,036

Adjust for sale: (200)

$$7,036 \times \frac{200}{1,500} =$$

		(938)	(938)
	1,300	6,098	5,063 (gain)

84 Stocks and Shares

Sale, 1/3/87:

Sale price (500 shares)   9,000

Pool brought forward

	Shares		Price
	1,300		6,098

Index to October, 1985:

$$6{,}098 \times \frac{95.59 - 95.23}{95.23} = 25$$

(0.004)

                                          6,123

27/10/85 purchase   400   7,000

                   1,700   13,123

Index to March, 1987:

$$13{,}123 \times \frac{103 - 95.59}{95.59} = 1{,}024$$

(0.078)

                                      14,147

Adjust for sale: (500)

                   1,200

$$\frac{14{,}147 \times 500}{1{,}700} =$$ (4,161)

                                        4,839 (gain)

b) The 1982 "pool" in which all the different purchases of the same share between 6th April, 1965 and 5th April, 1982 are aggregated and an average purchase price calculated. On a sale the new pool is deemed to be sold first (LIFO) and then shares from the 1982 pool.

Example

Gordon has the following purchases of shares of Linklater Holdings plc:

	Shares	Price
April, 1978	500	1,200
June, 1981	600	2,200
Value 31st March, 1982		£5 each
May, 1983	300	1,700
July, 1984	500	4,000

He sells 1,000 shares for £10,000 in August, 1985.

R.P.I. (Old index figures)

March, 1982	313.4
May, 1983	333.9
July, 1984	351.5
August, 1985 (say)	375

Calculation of gain: **Total**

Sale price, new pool (800 shares) $10,000 \times \dfrac{800}{1,000} = 8,000$

	Shares					**Price**
May, 1983	300					1,700

Indexation to July, 1984 $1,700 \times \dfrac{351.5 - 333.9}{333.9} = 91$

(0.053)

          1,791

July, 1984	500	4,000
	800	5,791

Indexation to Aug, 1985 $5,791 \times \dfrac{375 - 351.5}{351.4} = 388$ 6,179   1,821

(0.067)

Sale price, (982 holding (200 shares)) $10,000 \times \dfrac{200}{1,000} = 2,000$

	Shares	**Cost**
April, 1978	500	1,200
June, 1981	600	2,200
	1,100	3,400

$3,400 \times \dfrac{200}{1,100} = 618$

Indexation (using 31st March, 1982 value):

$200 \times 5 = 1,000 \times \dfrac{375 - 313.4}{313.4} = 197$ 815   1,185

(0.197)

          3,006

c) All purchases before 6th April 1965 are matched individually with sales on the LIFO basis unless an election has been made to include them in the 1982 pool (*see* later).

Capital distributions

Sometimes a special dividend arising out of a windfall profit to a company (such as on the sale of a capital asset) is described as a "capital distribution" or "capital dividend". This type, however, is normally the subject of an income tax Schedule F charge and is not relevant to capital gains tax. To be a capital gains tax matter there must be a repayment of share capital in whole or in part. In practice this mainly occurs when a company is being liquidated. (*S*.233(2)), *ICTA*.70).

86 Stocks and Shares

When a person receives a capital distribution it is treated as a disposal of an interest in shares, and therefore, a capital gain/loss arises. (S.72).

The calculation in general will be as for a part disposal.

If however the distribution is regarded as "small" (i.e. does not exceed 5% of the value of the entire asset) the Inspector is empowered not to assess any gain, but deduct the distribution from the cost of the shares, thus delaying the assessment to any future sale. (S.72(2)). See the paragraphs on rights issues for an example.

Capital distribution includes any distribution which is not income in the hands of the recipient.

Any disposal of "rights" is also treated as a capital distribution. (S.73). See later paragraphs for fuller details.

Example

A company repays part of its share capital. Bloggs, a shareholder, is left in the following position:

Original number of shares owned 800 for which he paid £500.

200 shares are repaid with a capital distribution of £250.

The remaining 600 are valued at £700 after the capital distribution.

Disposal value		250
Less: Apportioned cost $500 \times \dfrac{250}{250+700} =$	131	
Indexation allowance (say)	10	141
Assessable gain		109

A reorganisation of a company's share capital (Ss.77, 78 & 79)

This general heading covers two main types of action:

1. The allotment of shares (or even debentures) to shareholders in proportion to their holdings either with payment (a rights issue), or without payment (bonus or scrip issue).

2. The amendment of rights attaching to one class of share where there is more than one class.

The general rule in both cases is that either form of reorganisation is not a disposal, but the new shares acquired are treated as being received at the same time as the originals and for the same cost plus any additional price paid on the reorganisation.

"Original shares" are defined in the Act as those held before the reorganisation, and "new shares" as those held after, and may include some or all of the originals.

Stocks and Shares 87

Bonus and rights issues

A bonus issue is merely a free distribution of new shares. It adds nothing to the value of the total share capital, but merely dilutes the average value per share. The new shares are treated as being acquired at the same date and price as the originals.

Example

In 1979 a person buys 2,000 ordinary shares in ABC Ltd. for £3,000 (including expenses).

In 1980 there is a bonus issue of 1 for 4.

In 1987 he sells 800 of the shares for £4,000 (excluding expenses).

The calculation is:

Sale price		4,000
Less: Purchase price $3,000 \times \dfrac{800}{2,500} = 960$		(1,360)
Indexation from March 1982 (say)	400	
Gain		2,640

Cost of remaining $1,700 = 3,000 - 960 = 2,040$

A rights issue is treated the same. The only difference is that the purchase price is now the original cost plus any additional payment for the rights.

Example

Taking the example above, the issue of 1 for 4 in 1980 was a rights issue not a bonus issue, with £1 per share being paid for each new one.

The calculation now becomes:

			£		£
Sale price	(of 800 shares)				4,000
Less: Cost of	2,000 shares	3,000			
Plus:	500 (1 for 4)	500			
	2,500	$3,500 \times \dfrac{800}{2,500} = 1,120$			
Indexation (*see* later) (say)				440	(1,560)
			Gain		(2,440)

Cost of remaining $1,700 = 3,500 - 1,120 = 2,380$

For indexation purposes any new consideration given for the new shares is treated as expenditure incurred on the date it is actually paid, and not deemed to be incurred at the same time as the original cost.

88 Stocks and Shares

Example

A man acquired 1,000 ordinary shares in Anything plc for £5,000 on 20, May, 1983. On 17, August, 1983 there was a rights issue of one new share for each ten held at a cost of £1 per new share. He sold 300 shares for £3,600 on 9, September, 1987.

Assume RPI:

May, 1983	84.64
August, 1983	85.68
September, 1987 (say)	108.00

Sale price			3,600
Cost		5,000	
Indexation allowance $5,000 \times \dfrac{108-84.64}{84.64} = 1,380$ (0.276)			6,380
Cost of rights issue		100	
Indexation allowance $\dfrac{108-85.68}{85.68} = 26$ (0.261)			126
			$6,506 \times 300 = 1,775$
			1,100
Gain			1,825

If there has been more than one purchase of a particular share, the bonus or rights issue is allocated amongst the purchases proportionately. If one purchase was before 6th April, 1965, this will necessitate a revised valuation on that day, and this is generally easily obtained from one of several reference books, at least for quoted securities. (Moodies, Extel, etc.)

Example

Illustrating the effect of a rights issue, with a purchase before 6th April, 1965.

In 1963 a person buys 1,000 ordinary shares in ABC Ltd. for £1,200 (including expenses) and in 1968 a further 500 shares for £1,000 (including expenses).

On 6th April, 1965 the value was originally £1.60 per share.

In 1970 there is a rights issue of 1 for 2 at a price of £1.50 per share, which the shareholder takes up. The recalculated value of 1,500 shares deemed purchased before 6th April, 1965 is £1.57 per share.

In 1988 he sells 2,000 shares for £8,000 (excluding expenses). He has elected to be assessed on the pooling basis under paragraph 3, Schedule 5. (See later concerning this).

Stocks and Shares 89

The calculation is:

			£
2,000 shares sold for			8,000
Less: Pool price			
1965 1,500×£1.57		2,355	
1968 500 purchased for	1,000		
Plus: 250×£1.50=	375	1,375	
2,250 shares cost		3,730	
2,000 cost 3,730×2,000 / 2,250	=	3,315	
Indexation (say)		1,000	(4,315)
		Gain	3,685

If there have been different purchases of the same share before and after April 1982, and then there is a rights issue, the new shares have:
1. To be allocated *pro rata* to the respective 1982 and new pools.
2. When sold:
   a) Treated as a new acquisition in the new pool to calculate the indexation.
   b) The cost of the original shares and the rights issue in the 1982 pool have to be separated and indexed separately (from 31st March, 1982 and the date was paid for the rights issue, respectively).

Example
Gregory has the following transactions in the shares of Widget Enterprises, plc £1 ordinary shares.

Transactions	Date	No. of Shares	Price (£)
Buy	Feb. 1980	200	1,500
Buy	Nov. 1981	600	4,000
Value	March, 1982	Per share	10
Buy	January, 1985	400	5,600
Rights issue	Nov. 1986	1 for 4 held	12 per new share
Sell	March, 1988	700	21,000

The rights issue was allocated as follows:

New pool:

	Shares		Cost
Jan. 1985	400		5,600
Rights issue	100	100×12 =	1,200

90 Stocks and Shares

1982 pool:

	Shares	**Cost**
Feb. 1980	200	1,500
Nov. 1981	600	4,000
	800	5,500

Nov, 1986 rights issue	200	$200 \times 12 =$	2,400

RPI:	March 1982	79.44
	Jan. 1985	91.20
	Nov. 1986	99.29
	March 1988 (say)	120.00

On the sale of 700 shares for £21,000 (£30 per share) in March 1988 the calculation of the gain is:

New pool:

Sale of 500 shares × £30 = 15,000

	Shares	**Cost**
Jan 1985	400	5,600

Index to Nov. 1986:

$$\frac{5,600 \times 99.29 - 91.20}{91.20} = \quad 499$$

(0.089) 6,099

Rights issue	100	1,200
	500	7,299

Index to March 1988:

$$\frac{7,299 \times 120 - 99.29}{99.29} = \quad 1,526 \qquad (8,825) \qquad 6,175$$

(0.209)

1982 pool:

Of the 200 shares sold (700 sold − 500 from new pool) divide between original purchases and rights issue:

$$200 \times \frac{800 \text{ (original)}}{1,000 \text{ (total)}} = \quad 160 \text{ originals sold}$$

$$200 \times \frac{200 \text{ (rights issue)}}{1,000 \text{ (total)}} = \quad 40 \text{ rights issue sold}$$

$200 \times £30 =$ 6,000

$$\text{Cost } 5,500 \times \frac{200}{800} = \quad 1,375$$

Index (at March, 1982 value) to
March 1988:

$160 \times 10 = 1{,}600 \times \dfrac{120 - 79.44}{79.44}$ =   818   2,193

(0.511)

40 rights issue $\times 12$ =   480

Index (from Nov. 1986)

$480 \times \dfrac{120 - 99.29}{99.29}$ =   100   580   (2,773)   3,227

(0.209)

Total gain   9,402

Disposal of bonus and rights issue

When a shareholder becomes entitled to a bonus or rights issue, he may not
wish, for one reason or another, to hold on to or even take up the entitlement.
He may therefore be willing to dispose of the entitlement. If he does, then:
1. It is a part-disposal of the entire holding involving an apportionment of the
cost price using the part-disposal formula.
2. The part-cost is, of course, suitably indexed.

Example

Hall bought 1,000 shares (for £8,000) in Goblin Enterprises plc in November,
1984. He became entitled to a rights issue in May 1987. New shares can be
acquired for £5 per share for each 2 shares already held. However, Hall does
not wish to take up the rights issue and therefore sells the entitlement for £2,700.
The value of each share after the rights issue was £8.50 per share.

RPI: Nov. 1984   90.95

           May 1987 (say)   104.00

Sale price (amount received for sale of entitlement)   2,700

Apportioned cost $8{,}000 \times \dfrac{2{,}700*}{2{,}700 + 8{,}500 = 11{,}200}$ = 1,929

Indexation $1{,}929 \times \dfrac{104 - 90.95}{90.95}$ (0.143) = $\underline{276}$ (2,205)

Gain   495

*Note: The part-disposal formula is made up of: 2,700, the sale price of the
rights; 11,200, the total value of the holding on the day after the rights issue:
2,700, sale price plus 8,500 (1,000 shares still held valued at £8.50 per share).

If the sale price of the bonus/rights entitlement is five per cent or less of the
total value of the holding after the rights issue, then instead of having a capital
gain the taxpayer can elect to deduct the sale price from the cost price carried

92 Stocks and Shares

forward. This is known as the "small disposal" formula. In the example above, for instance, the £2,700 sale price would have to be five per cent or less of the value of the holding after the rights issue − £11,200 × 5% = £560. (Note, the value is the denominator of the part-disposal formula). In this case, it could not be claimed.

Example

Carson buys 1,000 shares in Portibel plc for £5,000 in December 1985. He becomes entitled to a rights issue in June 1987 under which he can purchase one new share at £3 for each four shares held. He disposes of the entitlement for £780. After the rights issue each share is worth £25.

RPI:	Dec. 1985		96.05	
	June 1987 (say)		104.00	
Sale price				780
Cost	$5,000 \times \dfrac{780}{780+25,000} = \dfrac{780}{25,780}$		= 152	
Indexation	$152 \times \dfrac{104-96.05}{96.05}$	(0.083) =	13	(165)
Gain				615

But:

As the sale price received, £780, is less than five per cent of the total value (5% = 25,780 = £1,289), the taxpayer could, if he wishes, claim a form of rollover relief of the sales price instead of having a capital gain of £615.

Therefore:

Cost price		5,000
Indexation to date of 5,000 × 0.083 =		415
Rights issue (June, 1987)		5,415
Sale price received		(780)
Cost price carried forward (and no capital gain)		4,635

However, if the gain (£615) is not chargeable to tax, because of, for example, the annual exemption, the taxpayer would be better off accepting the capital gain instead of claiming the rollover relief.

Conversion of securities (S.82)

The arrangements for the identification of new holdings arising from company reorganisations with the original shares apply generally to the conversion of securities:

1. Conversion of securities into shares.
2. Conversion taken optionally in place of cash.
3. Securities taken for shares on nationalisation and would include government or other public securities.

Stocks and Shares 93

Reorganisation of rights attaching to shares (S.81 and others)

When there is a complete reorganisation of the shares of a company and there is more than one class of new shares, a different rule applies to the apportionment of the original cost price of the old shares to the new shares, depending on whether the new shares are quoted or unquoted on a stock exchange. If quoted (or even only one of them is quoted) the cost is apportioned by reference to the respective market values on the first day on which the new shares are quoted. If unquoted, the apportionment is by reference to the values at the date of the first disposal of any of the shares.

It is first of all necessary to apportion the original cost among the reorganised shares by their respective values and then divide this apportioned cost by number of shares sold compared with the number held.

Example
Illustrating a conversion of securities showing the calculation where the shares are quoted.

In 1977 a person buys 2,000 £1 ordinary shares in ABC plc for £2,800 (including expenses).

In 1980 there is a reorganisation of share capital. Every share held is exchanged for one 50p ordinary and two 50p debentures.

In 1985 he sells 400 of the 50p ordinary for £700.

The 50p ordinary shares are quoted. Their values on the first day of quotation were:

2,000 50p Ordinary	3,000
4,000 50p Debentures	3,000
	6,000

Sale price	700

Less apportioned cost:

Cost	2,800
Indexation (say)	280

$$\frac{3,080 \times 3,000}{6,000} = 1,540 \times \frac{400}{2,000} = \quad 308$$

Gain	392

Remaining cost carried forward.
1,600 ordinary £1,232 (1,540−308)
4,000 debentures £1,540

94 Stocks and Shares

Company amalgamations and takeovers

For various reasons companies, from time to time, amalgamate or are the subject of a takeover bid. For tax purposes three distinct situations can be identified, all with special rules for postponement or relief from capital gains tax. The three situations are:

1. A takeover of one company by another, either the original company becoming a subsidiary of or amalgamated with the latter.

2. A company reconstruction when one or more new companies take over the business of the original which is then generally liquidated.

In both these cases the shareholders of the original company have a technical disposal of their shares, generally exchanging them for shares in the new company or companies.

3. The original company may also have a disposal of its business assets, (particularly land, buildings and goodwill) if they are taken into ownership by the other company or companies.

In all three cases the capital gain can be postponed, by applying the principle of "rollover" relief to when the new company shares/assets are eventually disposed of provided two general conditions (and others specific to each case) are complied with:

1. Only shares are exchanged for shares and no cash exchanges hands.

2. The schemes of arrangement, etc. are for bona fide commercial reasons, and tax avoidance is not one of the main aims.

Exchange of shares

When, on a takeover, etc., the shares of one company are exchanged for shares in another, a form of "rollover" relief is applied (so that the exchange is not itself a chargeable disposal, the gain being deferred until the new shares are disposed of) provided two conditions are satisfied:

1. The company issuing the new shares holds or acquires more than 25% of the ordinary share capital of the company concerned or acquire control as a result of a general offer made to all the shareholders.

2. The deal is for bona fide commercial reasons, and not part of a tax avoidance scheme. In cases of doubt an application can be made to the Inland Revenue for clearance on this point. Any relief due to persons holding 5% or less of the shares is unaffected by this condition.

When the conditions are satisfied, the new shares received are treated as having been acquired at the same time and the same price as the original shares.

Example

In 1978 Smart buys 1,400 25p ordinary shares in Bank Properties Ltd. for £3,725. In 1979 they are taken over by Insurance Land & Property Ltd., each 25p ordinary share in Bank Properties Ltd. being exchanged for one ordinary Insurance L & P Ltd. 30p share (valued at 45p after the takeover), and £3 of

Stocks and Shares 95

8% debenture loan stock in Insurance L & P Ltd. (valued at £2.95 for £3 nominal after the takeover). In 1985 Smart sells the £4,200 (nominal) of debenture loan stock for £6,730. All the shares and securities are quoted on the stock exchange.

The original value of £3,725 was split on takeover:

1,400 30p ordinary Insurance

$$\text{L \& P Ltd.} = 3,725 \times \frac{630^*}{4,760^{***}} \qquad = \qquad 493$$

£4,200 8% debentures Insurance

$$\text{L \& P Ltd.} = 3,725 \times \frac{4,130^{**}}{4,760} \qquad = \qquad 3,232$$

$$3,725$$

Notes:

* £630 is the value of 1,400 ordinary 30p shares (at 45p each) after takeover.

** £4,130 is the value of £4,200 debentures (at £2,95 per £3 nominal) after the takeover.

*** £4,760 is the total value of the bid (£630+£4,130)

The assessable gain is therefore:

Sale price		6,730
—Deemed cost	3,232	
Indexation (say)	400	3,632
Gain		3,098

Smart retains the 1,400 ordinary shares with a deemed cost of £493.

Scheme of reconstruction (Ss.85 & 86).

The same kind of rollover relief is also available (subject, again, to being for bona fide commercial reasons, and no cash changing hands) when, under a scheme of company reconstruction a company or companies issue shares or securities to shareholders of another company and the original shares are retained or cancelled. This is in practice done when the family controlling a company disagree about how to run it and wish to split it up amongst the separate branches of the family so that each can then go their separate way (see the next example below).

There is no indexation allowance calculated at the time of the reorganisation, etc. but any further consideration paid is deemed to be incurred on the actual day of the reorganisation for this purpose, it is not deemed to be part of the original expenditure.

96 Stocks and Shares

Transfer of assets between companies on a reconstruction or amalgamation
(S.267, *TA*, 1970)

In a company takeover or reconstruction sometimes the assets of the original company are taken over by the new company or companies. Provided the scheme fulfills certain conditions, there is no disposal by the original company, the assets passing to the new company at the original cost price for capital gains purposes. The conditions are:

1. The scheme is for bona fide commercial purposes. Again, application can be made to the Inland Revenue for clearance in doubtful cases.

2. The whole of the assets and liabilities are transferred.

3. No other consideration is paid for the transfer of the assets.

4. Both companies are resident in the UK.

An indexation allowance is calculated on the transfer from company to company to compute the acquisition value of the new company. The new company does not have to keep the asset for twelve months before another indexation allowance can be calculated. Any loss incurred by the new company can be reduced by the amount of the original indexation allowance.

Example

Vanilla Flavourings Ltd. is a private company founded by Giuseppe Flavori in 1967. He has now retired, and the business is now run by Pietro and Juan who cannot agree on how to develop it. Therefore, it is decided to form two new companies, Rent-a-Cornet Ltd., and Waferthin Ltd. One company is wholly owned by one son and his family, and will take over the entire assets and liabilities of Vanilla Flavourings, splitting them equally between the two new companies. The details are:

Vanilla Flavourings Ltd:

Assets:	*Value*	*Cost*
	£	£
Premises	200,000	80,000
Goodwill	60,000	Nil
Plant & Machinery	40,000	70,000
Stock	63,000	50,000
Debtors	20,000	—
	383,000	
Liabilities	110,000	
Net value	273,000	

The shares are owned by:		*Original acquisition value*
		£
Pietro & family	500	67,000
Juan & family	500	67,000
Total issued	1,000	134,000

The original shares of Vanilla Flavourings Ltd were issued for £134,000 value and with "rollover" relief the shares of the acquiring companies would have the same value adjusted for indexation of the original values.

On the reconstruction the two new companies each acquire half the assets and liabilities (with the original costs of premises and goodwill for capital gains purposes. No other assets are generally liable to capital gains tax). Vanilla Flavourings has no assessable disposal on relinquishing the premises and goodwill.

The new shares in the new companies each have a total deemed acquisition value of £67,000, split appropriately between the shares issued.

Reorganisations where part of distribution is in cash

On a reorganisation of share capital when part of the distribution is in cash, such as in a takeover bid, the cash portion is treated as a sale of part of the original holding, and the normal part disposal rules apply.

Example

Illustrating the situation on a takeover where part of the takeover bid is in cash.

Bloggs holds 2,000 shares in A Ltd. which originally cost him £6,000. B Ltd. makes a successful takeover bid for A Ltd. and Bloggs' shares are exchanged for 2,000 shares in B Ltd. (Market value £8,000) and £2,000 in cash.

$$\text{Disposal value (cash received)} \qquad 2,000$$

Less: Apportioned cost:

$$6,000$$
$$\text{Indexation (say)} \qquad 600$$

$$6,600 \times \frac{2,000}{2,000 + 8,000} \qquad = \qquad 1,320$$

$$\text{Gain} \qquad 680$$

Remaining cost carried forward.

$$\text{2,000 B Ltd. shares at } 6,600 - 1,320 = 5,280$$

Small distributions (S.72(2) & (5))

When there is an assessable capital distribution which is "small" compared with the value of the shares in respect of which it is made, it is not treated as a chargeable disposal, but is "rolled over" by deducting the amount of the distribution from the total deemed cost of the shares carried forward. We have earlier seen the same principle applied to the disposal of an entitlement to a rights issue. The same treatment can also be applied when cash is received as part of a reorganisation of share capital in a takeover bid, etc.

98 Stocks and Shares

Example

Jones purchased 3,000 shares in McHamish (Whisky Distillers) Ltd. for £4,670 in 1978. A successful takeover bid was made by the O'Flaherty Hooch Corporation in 1986 offering 2 O'Flaherty shares (value £1.70 each) and 16p in cash for each McHamish Ltd. share.

Disposal value (cash received) — 480

− Apportioned cost

$$5,000 \times \frac{480}{480 + 10,200^*} = 225$$

where apportioned cost is

	4,670
Indexation (say)	330

Assessable gain — 255

Carry forward 6,000 O'Flaherty shares at a cost of — 5,000

− 225

4,775

Note:* £10,200 is the value of the O'Flaherty shares
6,000 shares (2 for each McHamish share)
× £1.70 = £10,200

But £480 is less than 5% of $480 + 10,200 = 10,680 \times 5\% = £534$, so therfore small disposal treatment could be claimed, in which case:

Assessable gain — Nil

Carry forward 6,000 O'Flaherty shares at a cost of — 5,000

− 480

4,520

Shares held at 6th, April, 1965

General

6th, April, 1965 was the date capital gains tax was introduced, and as already mentioned earlier in the book, special rules apply to assets acquired before then to ensure only the gain accruing after 6th, April, 1965 is subject to capital gains tax. Special rules apply to shares and securities quoted on a recognised stock exchange and the normal rules of calculation to unquoted shares but, inevitably, with some exceptions. To summarize the rules before they are examined in detail:

Quoted shares and securities. The treatment depends on whether the taxpayer has made an appropriate election or not (para 3, Sch 5). This election is dealt with in more detail later on.

1. If no election has been made, then shares required prior to 6th April, 1965 are treated separately from shares acquired after that date. On the disposals up

Stocks and Shares   99

to 6th April, 1982 pre-April, 1965 disposals were the first deemed to be sold (FIFO), then on disposals from 6th April, 1982 to 5th April, 1985, the last, deemed to be sold (LIFO), and for disposals on or after 5th April, 1985 FIFO once more applies. (1st April not 6th April applies to disposals by a company).

Any actual gain is calculated as the smaller gain using the alternative of deducting either:

a) Original cost; or

b) Value at 6th April, 1965

both being suitably indexed.

If one produces a gain the other a loss, it is written off as neither gain or loss.

2. If any election has been made, the shares are deemed to have been acquired on 6th April, 1965 at their value on that day, and are then "pooled" as part of the "1982 holding."

The 1985 Finance Act gives taxpayers still owning quoted shares acquired before April, 1965 a fresh opportunity to elect for pooling as if the shares were acquired on 6th April, 1965 at their value on that date and include them. in the 1982 holding.

On valuing shares at 6th April, 1965 only the "half up" rule is used, never the "quarter up" rule (para 3, Sch.6).

Unquoted shares are treated the same, except that no election for pooling into the "1982 holding" is available.

1. The shares acquired prior to 6th April, 1965 are or were deemed to be:

a) First disposed of on disposals up to 5th April, 1982.

b) Last to be disposed of on disposals between 6th April, 1982 and 5th April, 1985.

c) First to be disposed of on disposals from 6th April, 1985.

Substitute 1st April, for 6th April, when dealing with corporate holdings of shares.

2. The gain or loss is calculated on the alternative of:

a) Deducting the original cost (index-linked) and then "time- apportioning" the gain (or loss).

b) Deducting the value at 6th April, 1965 (index-linked).

If one produces a gain and one a loss, it is written off as a nil "no gain/no loss" situation.

Quoted securities held on 6, April, 1965

The calculation of gains or losses on the disposal of securities will depend on whether or not an election has been made under paragraph 3, Sch.5. The rules contained in this chapter apply to all disposals made after 20th March, 1968, as amended by Finance Act, 1982, and the indexation rules.

100 Stocks and Shares

When no election has been made

The shares, etc. purchased prior to 6, April, 1965 are deemed (since 6th April, 1985) the last to be disposed of, and then on a LIFO (last in, first out) basis.

The shares when deemed to be disposed of are not pooled. The gain is calculated on the basis of the lower of:

1. original cost without time apportionment

AND

2. 6, April, 1965 value.

Both are index-linked as necessary. No taxpayers' election is needed for 6, April, 1965 value to apply. If one method produces a gain and another a loss, then the result is no gain/no loss.

Example

A man dealt in the ordinary shares of XYZ plc as follows:

Transaction	Date	Number of Shares	Price (£)
Buy	20/ 7/61	200	200
Buy	18/ 9/62	400	900
Value at	6/ 4/65		£1.50 per share
Buy	7/10/75	300	800
Value at	31/ 3/82		£4 per share
Buy	8/ 5/82	200	1,100
Sell	29/ 7/85	1,000	6,000

Assume RPI (old index figures)

March, 1982	313.4
May, 1982	318
April, 1985	363
July, 1985	400

1. Assuming no pooling election: **Total**

New holding (200 shares) $6{,}000 \times \dfrac{200}{1{,}000} =$ 1,200

Cost 1,100

Indexation $1{,}100 \times \dfrac{400 - 363}{363}$ 113   1,213   (13)

(0.102)

1982 holding (300 shares) $6{,}000 \times \dfrac{300}{1{,}000} =$ 1,800

Cost 800

Indexation (using 31/3/82 value)

$300 \times 4 = 1{,}200 \times \dfrac{400 - 313.4}{313.4}$ 332   1,132   668

(0.276)

Stocks and Shares 101

Sept, 1962 purchase (400 shares) 6,000 × $\dfrac{400}{1,000}$ = 2,400

Cost	900 6/4/65 value 400×1.50 =	600
Cost		900
Indexation 400×4=1,600×0.276 =		442	1,342	1,058

July, 1961 purchase (100 shares) 6,000 × $\dfrac{100}{1,000}$ = 600

Cost 200 × $\dfrac{100}{200}$ = 100

Indexation 100×4=400×0.276 = 111 211 389

2,102

2. Assuming a pooling election has been made:
Newholding (13)
1982 holding (800 shares) 6,000 × $\dfrac{800}{1,000}$ = 4,800

	Shares		Price
6/4/65	600	600×1.50=	900
7/10/75	300		800
	900		1,700 × $\dfrac{800}{1,000}$ = 1,360

Indexation (using 31/3/82 value)
800×4 = 3,200×0.276 = 884 2,244 2,556

2,543

When an election has been made
With the making of the election the original purchases price of shares bought before 6th April, 1965, is ignored for all purposes. They are taken at their valuation on that date and pooled with all purchases of the same shares up to 5, April, 1982 and an average pool price calculated.

The form of the election
The election can be made for securities in one or both of two categories, a separate election being needed for the election

The election can be made for securities in one or both of two categories, a separate election being needed for each. Once an election has been made it covers all shares in that category and not just the shares of any particular company. Once it has been made it is irrevocable and covers all present and future transactions.

The election must be in writing to the Inspector not later than two years after the end of the year of assessment in which the first relevant disposal is made.

102 Stocks and Shares

More time may be allowed at the Revenue's discretion. The first "relevant disposal" is the first sale in either category after 19th March, 1968.

If shares are held by one person in more than one capacity i.e. as an individual and also as a trustee, a separate election is required for each capacity. For a group of companies an election made by the parent covers all subsidiary companies as well.

The two groups of shares for which elections can be made are:

1. Fixed interest and preference shares.

2. All others, being in the main ordinary shares and all shares which participate in the profits of the company at other than a fixed rate of dividend.

Unquoted shares and securities held at 6th April, 1965 (para.13, Sch.5)

The gains or losses on the disposal of such shares are calculated on the time apportionment formula and not included in any pooling arrangements. The pooling arrangements apply, of course, to unquoted shares purchased after 6th April, 1965.

When unquoted shares held at 6th April, 1965 have been part of a re-organisation of share capital, however, special rules apply and these are dealt with in Appendix 2.

If the taxpayer wants to claim the valuation at 6th April, 1965 he can do so within the normal two year limit. If he does so, the valuation of the shares is done in accordance with the normal market value rules contained within S.150. The Revenue have a special department, the Shares Valuation Division, which deals with share valuations, this is not normally the job of the local inspector.

An election for valuation at 6th April, 1965 is irrevocable, once made. As the Inland Revenue will only discuss the valuation of shares at 6th April, 1965 AFTER the election has been made, a decision to make such an election must be considered very carefully before actually making it, as if the taxpayer or his advisers get the values wrong, the mistake cannot afterwards be rectified.

The valuation of unquoted shares is a complicated topic, and too specialised for this book. Readers should consult a specialist book on this.

Appeals or questions of value of unquoted shares arising from 13th March, 1975 are heard only by the Special Commissioners.

Example

Bernard has the following transactions in the £1 ordinary shares of Bemused Co. Ltd., an unquoted trading company.

Stocks and Shares 103

Transaction	Date	No. of shares	Price £
Buy	6 April 1959	100	3,000
Buy	6 April 1960	150	4,000
Value	6 April 1965	per share	40
Buy	6 April 1970	50)	6,000
Buy	6 April 1974	70)	Pooled 7,000
		120	13,000
Value	31 March 1982		£150 per share
Buy	4 June 1982	10	1,000
Buy	6 May 1983	20	5,000
Buy	9 November 1983	30	4,000
Sell	6 April 1986	380	133,000
			(Average per share £350)

Retail price index (assumed) (old index)

March, 1982	313.4
June, 1982	322.9
May, 1983	333.9
November, 1983	341.9
April, 1986	440

Computation of capital gain: **Total**

Sale of new holding (60 shares) $133,000 \times \dfrac{60}{380} = $ 21,000

	Shares		Price
June, 1982	10		1,000
Index to May, 1983		$1,000 \times \dfrac{333.9-322.9}{322.9}$ (0.034) $= 34$	
			1,034
May, 1983	20		5,000
	30		6,034
Index to Nov, 1983		$6,034 \times \dfrac{341.9-333.9}{333.9}$ (0.024) $= 145$	
			6,179
Nov, 1983	30		4,000
	60		10,179

104 Stocks and Shares

Index to
April, 1986 $10,179 \times \dfrac{440-341.9}{341.9}$ = 2,922   13,101   7,899
(0.287)

Sale of 1982 holding (120 shares)

$$133,000 \times \dfrac{120}{380} = 42,000$$

	Shares	**Price**
April, 1970	50	6,000
April, 1974	70	7,000
	120	13,000

Indexation (using 31/3/82 value)

$120 \times 150 = 18,000 \times \dfrac{440-313.4}{313.4}$ =   7,272   20,272   21,728
(0.404)

April, 1960 purchase (150 shares)

$$133,000 \times \dfrac{150}{380} = 52,500$$

Cost   4,000
Indexation $150 \times 150 = 22,500 \times 0.404 =$ 9,090   13,090

$39,410 \times \dfrac{21}{26}$ = 31,831

Sale price   52,500
6/4/65 value $150 \times 40 =$ 6,000
Indexation   9,090   15,090

37,410   31,831

April, 1959 purchase (50 shares)

$$133,000 \times \dfrac{50}{380} = 17,500$$

Cost $3,000 \times \dfrac{50}{100}$ = 1,500

Indexation $150 \times 150 = 7,500 \times 0.404 =$ 3,030   4,530

$12,970 \times \dfrac{21}{27}$ = 10,087

Sale price   17,500
6/4/65 value $50 \times 40 =$ 2,000
Indexation   3,030   5,030

12,470   10,087

71,545

If the share capital of the company has been reorganised, and shares were held on 6th April, 1965, special rules apply regarding the application of time-apportionment. See Appendix 2 for further details.

Compensation Stock

When shares in companies are acquired by compulsory purchase after 6th April, 1976 in exchange for government stock the following special rules now apply:

1. The takeover is not treated as an occasion of charge.
2. When the stock is subsequently sold the whole gain is not exempt as government stock held for more than twelve months. The gain is determined as follows:

(a) Any gain or loss in the old shares up to the date of exchange is relevant for capital gains.

(b) Any subsequent gains/loss on the sale of the government stock is ignored, if the twelve months rule is adhered to.

(c) Any chargeable gain on the compensation stock is not restricted by reference to the cost of the old shares if these were acquired prior to 6th April, 1965.

Example

Pratt acquired 1,000 shares in ABC Ltd. in 1968-69 for £5,000.

The company was nationalised in 1977-78 when he received £12,000 issue of government stock.

He sold this stock for £16,000 in 1980-81.

There is an assessable gain of $12,000 - 5,000 = 7,000$ in 1980-81.

The notional gains/losses are not relevant for capital gains when disposed of by:

(a) Personal representatives to beneficiaries.

(b) One spouse to another.

(c) Between members of a group of companies.

In these cases the person acquiring the shares is deemed to have acquired them at the same time as the person disposing of them.

Appendix 1 Disposal of shares and securities within a prescribed period of acquisition

All shares and securities acquired on the same day are treated as being acquired in a single transaction, and all shares disposed of on the same day are similarly treated as disposed of in a single transaction. The shares so acquired are identified as far as possible with shares so disposed of (S.66).

Certain transactions by companies (individuals are not affected) to establish losses have been stopped as from 14th April, 1975. They are (S.70):

106 **Stocks and Shares**

1. Selling and repurchasing the same shares ("bed and breakfast").
2. Purchasing a new block of shares and then selling part of the new, increased holding ("double banking").

The restriction applies when both the purchase and sale of shares of the same kind take place within a "prescribed period" (one month for shares disposed of through a stock exchange or ARIEL, and six months in any other case). The shares disposed of are identified with those acquired, and thus the loss is restricted to incidental costs of purchase and sale, provided the market price does not alter between the two transactions.

Any additional holding of gilts acquired (from 16th April, 1975) by any person (including both companies and individuals) within a "prescribed period" (one month for securities acquired through a stock exchange, six months in other cases) before a disposal of securities of the same kind are treated as reacquisition of the same securities. Any loss can only be set off against a gain on a subsequent disposal of the additional holding (S.70).

An additional rule introduced by the Finance Act, 1985 for identifying disposals and acquisitions of shares of the same class made within a period of ten days. When such shares sold are identified within acquisition in such circumstances the shares are excluded from new holding and no indexation given. This would effectively disallow any bed and breakfast arrangements, except when the entire holding was disposed of before the shares were repurchased (because the shares acquired would then constitute a different "new holding" from that which was extinguished on the disposal).

When the new pooling provisions apply, a person can have holdings of the same class of share, which he holds in the same capacity but which remain separate from the new holding. If he held any of the shares prior to 6th April, 1982 there may be a distinct 1982 holding. If any shares are still held, from before 6th April, 1965 (and not pooled in the 1982 holding, by election) these again are dealt with separately. To cater for this kind of case special rules of idenfication are used for disposals from 6th April, 1985.

Shares disposed of are identified first on a LIFO basis. These rules are subject to the rules described above regarding purchases and sales onthe same day. No specific statement as to identification of shares can override these rules.

Appendix 2 Reorganisation of unquoted shares held on 6th April, 1965 (Para.14, Sch.5)

When the shares of an unquoted company have been reorganised, and were held on 6th April, 1965, special rules apply to the computation of any future gain, but not if the reorganisation consists only of substituting shares of one class for those of another, whether more or less in number.

Stocks and Shares   107

If the reorganisation took place before 6th April, 1965, but after the shares had been acquired, the time apportionment formula cannot be used, only the 6th April, 1965 value.

If the reorganisation was after 6th April, 1965 then the shares are treated as being sold and reacquired on the date of the reorganisation. The gain up to the date of the reorganisation is calculated as usual, by time apportionment or 6th April, 1965 value. The gain from the reorganisation to the sale is calculated separately as if a purchase had taken place at the time of the reorganisation.

Example

Booth owns shares in Elastic Lampstands Ltd., an unquoted company. He acquired 1,000 £1 ordinary for £800 on 6th April, 1960. The share capital of the company is reorganised and Booth acquires instead of each ordinary share:

1 50p ordinary share (giving him 1,000)

and 2 25p 8% non-voting preference shares (giving

him 2,000)

The reorganisation took place:

1. On 6th April, 1964. Value of share at 6th April, 1965:

50p ordinary 90p each, 25p preference 60p each.

2. On 6th October, 1967. Value of original shares at 6th April, 1965 was £2.10p each, (equivalent to one 50p ordinary (90p) and two preference (60p each) in 1).

Their value on 6th October, 1967 was:

50p ordinary £1.10p.

25p preference 80p

Eventually Booth sells his shares on 6th April, 1986:

1,000 50p ordinary for £2,000.

500 25p preference for £600.

The assessable gains are:

1. Assuming reorganisation took place on 6th April, 1964.

Only 6th April, 1965 value can be used:

		50p ordinary
Sale price		2,000
Less: 6/4/65 value 1,000×90p =	900	
Indexation (say)	270	1,170
	Gain	830
		25p preference
Sale price		600
Less: 6/4/65 value 500×60p =	300	
Indexation (say)	90	390
	Gain	210
	Total gain	£1,040

108 Stocks and Shares

2. Assuming reorganisation took place on 6th October, 1967.

        Gain to 6th October, 1967:

        Time apportionment:

	50p ordinary
Deemed sale price $1,000 \times £1.10 =$	1,100

Less: cost

$$\frac{800 \times 1,100 \text{ (value of ordinary on 6/10/67)}}{1,100+1,600 \text{ (value of 2,000 preference on 6/10/67)}}$$

$= 800 \times 1,100 =$	326

        2,700

Gain	774

	25p preference
Deemed sale price $500 \times 80p =$	400

Less: Apportioned cost

        800

     Less: 326

$$\frac{474 \times 500 \text{ (number sold)}}{2,000 \text{ (number held)}} =$$

	118
Gain	282

Total gain $1,056 \times 2\frac{1}{2}$ (6/4/65 to 6/10/67)

        $7\frac{1}{2}$ (6/4/60 to 6/10/67)

    = £352

	50p ordinary
6th April, 1965 value	
Deemed sale price	1,100

Less: 2,100 (value of £1 ordinary at 6/4/65)

$$\frac{\times 1,100}{2,700}$$

	856
Gain	244

	25p preference
Deemed sale price	400

Less: $1,244^* \times \dfrac{500}{2,000}$

	311
Gain	89

Total gain £244+£89=	333

Stocks and Shares 109

Gain from 6th October, 1967 to 6th April, 1986:

			ordinary
Sale price			2,000
Less: value at 6th October, 1967	1,100		
Indexation (say)	330		1,430
		Gain	570
			preference
Sale price			600
Less: value at 6th October, 1967	400		
Indexation (say)	120		520
		Gain	80

Total gain $570 + 80 = 650$

Still held are 1,500 25p preference shares with values of:
6th April, 1965 $1,244 \times 1,500 = £933$
$$\frac{1,244 \times 1,500}{2,000} = £933$$
6th October, 1967 $1,500 \times 80p = £1,200$
$*1,244 = 2,100 - 856$.

Original cost is now irrelevant, as 6th April, 1965 value has been used once, and must therefore be used in any future sales.

By concession, the application of these rules is not to assess any gain greater than the actual gain made on disposal of the shares.

The case of CIR v. Beveridge (STC 1979 592) determined that the above rules apply on a takeover of one company by another where the original shares were purchased prior to 5th April, 1965 and there is a subsequent sale of the new shares.

Revision questions

For all examples, the retail price index is assumed to be:

March 1982	79.44
April 1984	88.64
October 1985	95.59
May 1986	97.85
August 1987 (say)	110.00

110 **Stocks and Shares**

1. Bolsover acquired and sold £1 ordinary shares in Button Enterprises plc as follows. Calculate the gain on the disposal in August 1987.

Transaction	Date	No. of Shares	Price
Buy	Nov. 1981	500	1,500
Buy	Feb. 1982	600	1,200
Value	March 1982	per share	£3 each
Buy	April 1984	300	2,000
Sell	March 1985	200	1,800
Buy	May 1986	700	4,500
Sell	Aug. 1987	1,000	10,000

2. Jones acquired and sold 50p ordinary shares in Goldman plc as follows. Calculate the gain on the disposal in August 1987.

Transaction	Date	No. of shares	Price
Buy	Aug. 1981	400	1,000
Buy	Feb. 1982	600	1,200
Value	March 1982	Per share	£3 each
Buy	Oct. 1985	500	3,000
Selll	Aug. 1987	800	4,800

3. Green acquired and sold £1 ordinary shares in Mountain plc as follows. Calculate the gain on the disposal in August 1987.

Transaction	Date	No. of shares	Price
Buy	Nov. 1981	400	2,000
Value	March 1982	Per share	£6 each
Buy	Oct. 1985	200	4,000
Rights issue	May 1986	1 for 2 held	£5 per new share.
Sell	Aug. 1987	500	25,000

4. Bullock acquired and sold £1 ordinary shares in Jones plc as follows. Calculate the gain on the disposal in August, 1987:

Transaction	Date	No. of shares	Price
Buy	April 1984	1,000	6,000
Rights issue	Aug. 1987	1 for 4 held	£4 per new share.
Value	After rights issue	per share	£10 each.

Bullock did not take up the rights issue but sold the entitlement for £1,000.

Stocks and Shares 111

5. Gillard acquired and sold £1 ordinary shares in Budd plc as follows. Calculate the gain on the disposal in August 1987.

Transaction	Date	No. of shares	Price
Buy	March 1964	200	400
Value	April 1965	Per share	£5 each
Buy	March 1981	400	2,000
Value	March 1982	Per share	£15 each
Buy	Oct. 1985	500	7,000
Sale	Aug. 1987	1,000	10,000

Calculate the gain assuming:
  a) No election for pooling was made pre-April 1965 purchases was made.
  b) Such an election was made.

Answers

1. **Sale out of new pool**   **Gain**

Sale of 8000 shares: $10,000 \times \dfrac{800}{1,000} = $ 8,000

	Share			Price
April 1984	300			2,000
Sale March 1985	(200)	$2,000 \times \dfrac{200}{300} =$		(1,333)
	100			667

Index to May 1986:
$667 \times \dfrac{97.85 - 88.64}{88.64} =$ (70)
(0.104)   737

| May 1986 | 700 | | | 4,500 |
| | 800 | | | 5,237 |

Index to Aug. 1987:
$5,237 \times \dfrac{110 - 97.85}{97.85} =$ (650)   (5,887)   2,113
(0.124)

112   Stocks and Shares

Sale out of 1982 pool

Sale of 200 shares: $10{,}000 \times \dfrac{200}{1{,}000} =$ 2,000

	Shares	**Price**
Nov. 1981	500	1,500
Feb. 1982	600	1,200
	1,100	2,700

$2{,}700 \times \dfrac{200}{1{,}100} = 491$

Index to Aug. 1987:

Value in March 1982 $200 \times £3 = 600 \times \dfrac{110 - 79.44}{79.44} = 231$ (722)   1,278

   (0.385)

Gain   3,391

---

2. Sale out of new pool   **Gain**

Sale of 500 shares: $4{,}800 \times \dfrac{500}{800} =$ 3,000

Cost   3,000

Indexation $3{,}000 \times \dfrac{110 - 95.59}{95.59}$ (0.151) =   453   3,453   (453)

Sale out of 1982 pool:

Sale of 300 shares: $4{,}800 \times \dfrac{300}{800} =$ 1,800

Cost:	**Shares**	**Price**
Aug. 1981	400	1,000
Feb. 1982	600	1,200
	1,000	2,200

$2{,}200 \times \dfrac{300}{1{,}000} = 660$

Index to Aug. 1987:

Value at March 1982:

$300 \times £3 = 900 \times \dfrac{110 - 97.85}{79.44}$ (0.385) =   347   (1,007)   793

Net gain   340

3. Allocation of right issue   **Gain**

New pool:

	Shares		Cost		
Oct. 1985	200		4,000		

Index to May, 1986:

$$4{,}000 \times \frac{97.85 - 95.59}{95.59} \quad = \qquad 96$$

(0.024)

			4,096		
Rights issue (1 for 2): 100		$100 \times £5 =$	500		
	300		4,596		

1982 pool:

	Shares		Price		
Nov. 1981	400		2,000		
Rights issue (1 for 2): 200		$200 \times £5 =$	1,000		

Sale of new pool:

$$\text{Sale of 300 shares } 25{,}000 \times \frac{300}{500} = \qquad\qquad\qquad 15{,}000$$

Cost: 4,596

Index to Aug, 1987:

$$4596 \times \frac{110 - 97.85}{97.85} \quad (0.124) = \qquad 570 \qquad (5{,}166) \qquad 9{,}834$$

Sale from 1982 pool:

$$\text{Sale of 200 shares } 25{,}000 \times \frac{200}{500} = \qquad\qquad\qquad 10{,}000$$

Proportion of sales:

$$\text{Original shares } 400 \times \frac{200}{600} = \qquad 133$$

$$\text{Rights} \qquad\qquad 200 \times \frac{200}{600} = \qquad 67$$

$$\text{Original cost } 2{,}000 \times \frac{133}{400} = \qquad 665$$

Index (March 1982 value):

$$133 \times £6 = 798 \times 0.385^* = \qquad 307 \qquad 972$$

Rights issue 67×5 =   335

Index (from may, 1986):

$$335 \times \frac{110 - 95.59}{95.59}\,(0.151) \quad = \qquad 51 \qquad 386 \qquad (1{,}358) \qquad 8{,}642$$

Gain   18,476

*See above

114 Stocks and Shares

4. Sale price   1,000

$$\text{Cost } 6,000 \times \frac{1,000}{1,000+10,000 \ (1,000 \times £10)} = \quad 600$$

Index:

$$600 \times \underline{110-88.64} \ (0.241) \qquad = \quad 145 \qquad (745)$$

Gain   255

Small disposal rollover:
5% × 11,000 = £550, therefore rollover not available.

5. Sale out of new pool:

500 shares $10,000 \times \dfrac{500}{1,000} =$ 5,000

Cost   7,000

Index: $7,000 \times \dfrac{110-95.59}{95.59} \ (0.151) =$ 1,057   (8,057)   (3,057)

Sale out of 1982 pool

400 shares $10,000 \times \dfrac{400}{1,000} =$ 4,000

Cost   2,000

Index (at March 1982 value):

$400 \times 15 = 6,000 \times \dfrac{110-79.44}{79.64} \ (0.385) =$ 2,310   (4,310)   (310)

Sale out of pre-1965 purchase:

100 shares $10,000 \times \dfrac{100}{1,000} =$ 1,000

$\text{Cost } 400 \times \dfrac{100}{200} = \qquad\qquad 100$

April, 1965 value $100 \times 5 \quad = \qquad 500$

Index (at March, 1982 value):

$100 \times 15 = 1,500 \times 0.385 \quad = \qquad 578$ (1,078)   (78)

Total loss   (3,445)

Chapter Fifteen

Various Exemptions

Authorised unit trusts and investment trusts

Unit trusts are schemes covered by an order of the Department of Trade under S.17 of the Prevention of Fraud (Investments) Act, 1958.

An investment trust is a company fulfilling certain conditions (S.359, CGTA, 1979): it must not be a close company; it must be UK resident; it must derive its income from shares and securities; it must not distribute by way of dividend any gain arising from the sale of investments; it must not retain more than 15 per cent of its income derived from shares, etc., and it must be approved by the Board of Inland Revenue.

Both unit trusts and investment trusts are treated as companies for tax purposes and their units, etc as share capital in a company.

When a trust disposes of investments these are completely exempted from capital gains tax on any profit they make. (S.60, FA, 1980). However, this does not exempt their unit holders from liability when they dispose of units. There is liability in the ordinary way just as if a sale of units was a sale of ordinary company shares, profits being assessable and losses allowable.

Gilt-edged securities and corporate bonds

The disposal of gilt-edged securities or qualifying corporate bonds or any option or contract to acquire or dispose of them is exempt from capital gains tax. Gains are not assessable and losses are not allowable.

"Gilt-edged securities" are defined as those listed in Schedule 2 of CGTA, 1979. A "qualifying corporate bond" is (S.64, FA, 1984) any bond, debenture stock or loan stock, secured or unsecured, issued by any company, UK or foreign, or any public or local authority which filfills certain conditions.

1. The stock (or some other security or share of the company) has been quoted on a recognised stock exchange (including the USM) since the issue of stock.

2. The amount of stock is expressed in sterling and does not fluctuate according to changes in the value of sterling against other currencies.

3. The stock is not convertible into a foreign currency stock and is not redeemable in a foreign currency other than at the rate of exchange current at the time of redemption.

116 Various Exemptions

4. The debt on the stock represents a normal commercial loan. It is not a normal commercial loan if it is convertible into shares or securities of a different description or confers the right to acquire further shares or securities. Nor is it a normal commercial loan if the interest fluctuates according to company trading results or value of assets, or exceeds a reasonable commercial return, or if the amount repayable exceeds the amount lent and is more than is reasonable by comparison with the terms of issue of securities in the Stock Exchange Official List.

Securities issued by a group company to another member of the same 75 per cent group do not qualify.

Chapter Sixteen

Transfer of a Business to a Company
(S.123)

Transfer

When a sole trader or a partnership wish to transfer their business to a limited company, they will often transfer the ownership of the business assets to the company. That is technically a disposal for capital gains purposes if the assets transferred show a gain at that time and are chargeable business assets (e.g. land, buildings, and goodwill). Provided certain conditions (see below) are satisfied, this gain can be postponed by "rolling over" against the cost price of the shares issued by the company in exchange for the value of the business transferred — in effect, reducing the cost price of the shares by the chargeable gains made on the assets transferred.

Example

Fred Glumm sets up a business in 1974, manufacturing jokes to go inside Christmas crackers. In 1986 he transfers the business as a going concern, together with all the assets, to a newly formed company, Glumm (Sidesplitters) Ltd., in exchange for 67,400 £1 ordinary shares, all fully paid. He sold 10,000 of the shares for £60,000 in 1988.

The details of the assets are:

	Cost in 1974	Value on transfer to company in 1986		Chargeable gains
Land and buildings	20,000*	57,000		32,000**
Goodwill	Nil	15,000		14,000***
Plant and machinery	8,000	6,300	Exempt from	Nil
Stock	3,000	4,800	CGT or showing	Nil
Debtors	Nil	9,600	a disallowable	Nil
Cash	2,000	3,700	loss	Nil
		96,400		46,000
—Liabilities		29,000		
Net worth of company		67,400	(therefore 67,400 £1 ordinary shares issued).	

118 Transfer of a Business to a Company

*Land & Buildings	20,000	**57,000	***Indexation of
Indexation	5,000	(25,000)	1,000 based on
	25,000	32,000	31/3/82 value.

Fred Glumm could claim to rollover the gain of 46,000 as follows:

Actual cost of shares	67,400
—Rolled over gain	(46,000)
Deemed cost of shares for capital gains purposes	21,400

Chargeable gain on sale of £10,000 shares in 1988-89:

Sale price		60,000
—Apportioned cost $21,400 \times \dfrac{10,000}{67,400} =$	3,175	
Indexation (say)	1,000	(4,175)
Assessable gain		55,825

Carry forward 57,400 shares at a remaining cost of 21,400—3,175 = £18,225.

Conditions

The conditions to be satisfied are:

1. The business must be transferred by a person other than a company.

2. It must be transferred as a going concern together with all of its assets other than cash. In the example above, therefore, Fred Glumm could have kept the cash of £3,700 in 1986 and still have claimed this rollover relief. The cost price of his shares would than have been.

	67,400
—Cash	(3,700)
	63,700
—Rollover	(46,000)
Deemed cost	17,700

3. The business is transferred wholly or partly for shares issued by the company to the person transferring the business.

If the transfer of the business is paid for by the company with a mixture of shares and other assets (normally cash) then a proportion of the gain (proportionate to the assets other than shares) is assessable, and only the balance of the gain can be rolled over against the cost price of the shares. The gain to be rolled over is calculated by applying the fraction

A (value of shares given in exchange)

B (value of total assets given in exchange) against the total gain.

Transfer of a Business to a Company   119

Example

Jim Salad sets up in business (in 1973) as a self-employed purveyor of sandwiches to the city masses. In 1987 he transfers the business, together with all the assets other than cash, to a company Rent-A-Butty Ltd. in exchange for 72,900 £1 ordinary shares (fully paid) and £10,000 in cash.

The details are:

	Cost in 1973	Value on transfer to company	Chargeable gains
Land and buildings	20,000*	68,000	44,000**
Goodwill	Nil	21,000	19,000***
Plant and machinery	2,100	1,700	Nil
Stock	1,000	4,900	Nil
Debtors	Nil	2,300	Nil
Cash	4,000	Nil (£6,000 in the	Nil
		business was	
		97,900 retained by	63,000
—Liabilities		15,000 Jim)	
Net worth of company		82,900	

1. Assessable

$$\frac{63,000 \times 10,000}{82,900} \quad = \quad £7,600$$

2. Rolled over

$$\frac{63,000 \times 72,900}{82,900} \quad = \quad £55,400$$

(Note: the £6,000 business cash retained is not treated as part of the cash by which the assessable proportion of the gain is calculated).

$$63,000$$

Deemed cost of the 72,900 shares to be carried forward is:

		72,900
—Rolled over gain		55,400
Deemed cost of shares		17,500

*	20,000	**68,000 ***Indexation of
Indexation	4,000	−24,000 2,000 based on
	24,000	44,000 31/3/82 value

A rolled over gain cannot create a negative cost, and therefore if the gain exceeds the net cost of the shares, part of the gain may end up assessable.

120　Transfer of a Business to a Company

Example

A garage proprietor transfers his business to a limited company. He makes gains of:

Land & Buildings		88,000
Goodwill		40,000
Gross gains		128,000
Value of shares issued by company		
Gross assets taken over		260,000
Gross liabilities taken over		150,000
Cost of shares		110,000
Gross gains	128,000	
Rolled over	110,000	110,000
Gain assessable	18,000	
Net net of shares		Nil

Indexation allowance

When a business is transferred to a company in exchange for shares, an indexation allowance is calculated, if appropriate, in calculating the gain to be rolled over against the acquisition value of the shares.

Practical Aspects of transferring a business to a limited company

One of the disadvantages of claiming this relief is that *all* the assets of the business have to be transferred to the limited company's ownership. Once property is owned by a company and is later sold there can be a double charge to tax to release the sale money into the hands of the shareholders:

1. Corporation tax on the company on its realised gain.

2.a) Income tax on distributing the money to the shareholders/directors by way of a dividend or remuneration.

OR b) A further capital gain on paying out the shareholders, probably by way of liquidating the company.

Therefore the proprietor may be tempted to retain the land and buildings in his own name and transfer only the other assets to the company. However, by doing that he may have retained a tax advantage on the property, but has not transferred *all* the business assets and therefore is liable to capital gains tax on the other chargeable assets actually transferred to the company (generally in practice this means goodwill, as all other assets should be exempt).

One way round the dilemma may be to grant the business a lease on the building prior to the formation of the company and then transfer to the company the whole of the business assets including the *lease* on the building, but retaining the freehold interest in individual ownership, thus qualifying for the rollover relief but preserving the proceeds of any subsequent sale of the building from a double charge to tax.

Chapter Seventeen

Replacement of Business Assets
(S.115 to 121)

General

When a trader disposes of an asset used in his business, generally a chargeable gain or an allowable loss results. If there is a loss then it is allowed against any present or future chargeable gains. If there is a gain, however, it is possible for the trader to avoid an immediate assessment to tax if he makes a S.115 election and certain conditions are fulfilled.

Under the provisions of S.115, the gain on the old asset is deducted from the cost of any replacement instead of being assessed to tax. The process can then be repeated on the sale of the second asset and indefinitely until the asset is not replaced when the total gains on the series of assets is charged to tax.

Indexation allowance
When the gain to be rolled over is calculated on the asset to be replaced, an indexation allowance is calculated.

The replacement asset has to be held for over twelve months before another indexation allowance can be calculated on the net acquisition value.

Example
A trader buys shop A in 1977 for £29,000 and sells it in 1986 for £50,000 replacing it with shop B costing £57,000.

Assessable gain:		£
Sale price		50,000
Less: Cost	29,000	
Indexation allowance (say)	1,000	30,000
Gain on A		20,000
The gain is dealt with:		
Cost of new shop B		57,000
Less: Gain on old shop A		20,000
Deemed cost of B for capital gains purposes		37,000

Any gain on the sale of B could then be rolled over against any replacement by C, etc.

Arithmetical difficulties

Rollover relief does not generally apply when only part of the sale proceeds of an asset are spent on a replacement. If, however, the amount of the proceeds retained is less than the gain (whether or not the whole of the gain is chargeable to tax) the trade can elect to have part of the gain rolled over, and only be assessed on the cash retained.

Example

Liverpool Condiments Ltd. bought factory A in 1968 for £135,000 to manufacture top quality jam butties. They find the market becoming very sticky. They therefore sell factory A in 1988 for £210,000 and buy a smaller one (factory B) for £195,000.

Gross gain on sale of A:

Sale price		210,000
—Cost	135,000	
Indexation allowance (say)	5,000	140,000
Gross gain		70,000
Assessed (cash retained) 210,000—195,000=		15,000
Rolled over (against cost of B)		55,000
		70,000
Cost of B		195,000
—Rolled over gain		55,000
Deemed cost of B		140,000

If part of the sale price is retained (and not reinvested in the replacement) and the purchase of the original took place prior to 6th April, 1965, the cost with time-apportionment method can lead to difficulties on calculating the assessable gain. Effectively the cash retained is time-apportioned to calculate the gain which is assessable.

Example

Rookham and Strandham (Travel Agents) Ltd. purchased business premises for £39,000 on 6/4/60. The value on 6/4/65 was £43,000. They sold these premises for £65,000 on 6/4/86 and replaced them with other premises for £62,000.

Cost with time-apportionment			**6/4/65 value**	
Sale price		65,000		65,000
—Cost	39,000		Value	43,000
Indexation allowance			Indexation allowance	
(say)	1,000	40,000	(say)	1,103 44,103
		$25,000 \times {}^{21}\!/_{26}$		20,897
	=	20,192		

124 Replacement of Business Assets

The assessable gain is $65,000-62,000=3,000\times^{21}\!/_{26}=$		2,423
Rollover relief given is $20,192-2,423=$	17,769	
Cost of replacement	62,000	
—Rolled over gain	(17,769)	
Deemed cost of replacement	44,231	

There would be no problem if 6/4/65 value were used. Say the value then was £50,000 and the gain $65,000-50,000=15,000$.

Assessable gain=	$65,000-62,000$ =		3,000
Rollover on	$15,000-\;\;3,000$ =		12,000
Cost of replacement		62,000	
—Rollover		(12,000)	
Deemed cost of replacement		50,000	

Conditions to be satisfied

The conditions which have to be fulfilled are as follows:

1. The asset disposed of must have been used solely for the purposes of the trade throughout the period of ownership, or in the case of an asset disposed of after 11th April, 1978, used for the trade of the owner's "family company". This has the same definition as for the granting of retirement relief (S.124).

2. The new asset must be used in the same or a different trade carried on by the person claiming the relief (prior to 12th April, 1978 the old and new assets had to be used in the SAME trade). Effectively, all the trades carried on by one person are, for this purpose, treated as the same trade.

3. The old and new asset must be within one of the specified classes (see below), but both need not belong to the same class. For acquisitions before 20th April, 1971 it was necessary for the original asset and the replacement to belong to the same class.

4. The purchaser of the old asset and the vendor of the new are unaffected by the election.

5. The new asset is acquired within a period of twelve months before, or three years after the disposal of the old asset. The Inspector has discretion to extend this period. The period before 6th April, 1973 was twelve months before or after the disposal.

For the purposes of rollover relief, all the trades carried on by a group of companies are treated as one. Therefore relief is available when one member of the groups sells an asset and another buys the replacement, provided they do not buy and sell to other group members. (S.276, TA, 1970). However, this is not as important as it was from 12th April, 1978 onwards (see 2. above).

The specified classes of assets are as follows:

Class 1

(a) Land and buildings occupied and used for the purposes of the trade, except where the trade is land dealing and development, or providing services for the occupier of land in which the trader has an interest.

(b) Fixed plant and machinery which does not form part of a building or structure. Therefore movable plant and machinery (e.g. motor vehicles) do not seem to qualify.

Class 2

Ships.

Class 3

Aircraft.

Class 4

Goodwill.

Class 5

Hovercraft.

Since April, 1969 there has been a restriction where the replacement asset is a depreciating asset. This is dealt with later.

When a person carries on a trade in different areas, this is to be treated as a continuation of the same trade for *S*.33 purposes.

No relief is due unless the new asset was purchased for use in the trade and not to realise a gain.

Apportionments are required where:

1. The old asset was not used for the purposes of the trade throughout the period.

2. Where only part of an asset (e.g. a building) was used for business purposes.

Rollover relief also applies, as from 11th April, 1972, not only to persons carrying on a trade, but to trade protection associations or to any body whose main interest is the promotion of the interest of its members in carrying on their trade or profession. Where the replacement asset is purchased after 11th April, 1974, rollover also applied to unincorporated associations or other bodies liable to corporation tax being non-profit making bodies or whose main activities are non-profit making.

Depreciating assets (S.117)

The rollover provisions are restricted where what is acquired to replace an existing business asset is a "depreciating asset". This is defined as one with an estimated life of not more than fifty years, or where the useful life will be less than fifty years within ten years of purchase i.e. the estimated life on purchase does not exceed sixty years.

When this is the case, and the replacement takes place after 5th April, 1969, the gain on the first asset can only be deferred until the earliest of several alternative events. These are:

1. The taxpayer disposes of the replacement.

OR

126 Replacement of Business Assets

2. He ceases to use it in the trade.

OR

3. The expiration of ten years from the date of acquisition of the second asset.

In effect the gain is placed on one side (and not rolled over). The payment of tax is thereby postponed until the earliest happening of the three events listed.

If, however, a third asset is acquired which is not a depreciating asset, the first claim can be withdrawn and the gain set against the new acquisition, and thus the restriction will not be applied to the deferment of the gain.

Where a group is concerned, chargeable gains in one company can still be set against the cost of a new asset in another company. Where appropriate the liability arising in the shortest of the three relevant periods will be assessed upon the company holding the second asset at that time.

In effect the gain (on the original No. 1 asset) is not rolled over against the depreciating asset, (No.2 asset) but merely postponed until the disposal, etc. of the depreciating No.2 asset.

However, if within one year before and up to three years after the disposal of the original asset a non-depreciating asset (No.3 asset) is acquired to replace the original (No.1 asset), the postponement of the gain by the purchase of the depreciating (No.2) asset is cancelled, and proper rollover relief substituted against the non-depreciating No.3 asset.

Example

A company sells a factory (No.1 asset) for £100,000 on 1/10/82 (having cost £39,000 in 1970) making a gain of £60,000 (after indexation).

It is "replaced" by fixed plant and machinery on 2/12/82 which costs £120,000. The machinery is sold on 8/8/84 for £34,000.

There would be:

A chargeable gain arising on 8/8/84 of £60,000.

However, if a non-depreciating asset was purchased on or before 30/9/85 for more than £100,000 the gain could be rolled over against it and the assessment on 8/8/84 be cancelled.

Say another factory was purchased on 5/4/85 for £170,000 then:

Gross cost price	170,000
—Rolled over gain	60,000
Deemed cost of asset No. 3	110,000

Chapter Eighteen

Gift of Business Assets
(S.126 & Sch.4)

General

A capital gain arising on or after 12th April, 1978 from a gift or transfer at an undervalue of:
1. Business assets.
2. Shares in a family trading company.
3. Agricultural property not used by the transferor or his family company for the purposes of a trade provided the property would attract CTT relief is claimed, can be deferred by rolling it over against the acquisition cost of the transferee.

This relief is, of course, secondary to the general relief for gifts by one individual to another individual (see earlier).

Whilst there is still a business assets gifts relief, it has now largely been overtaken by the general gifts relief. It now only really applies when an individual makes a gift of business assets to a U.K. resident company. If the general gifts relief can apply, it takes precedence over business gifts relief.

Indexation applies as to the general gift relief.

Arithmetic

1. On a gift the whole gain is rolled over, but on a sale at undervalue the rollover relief is limited to the amount of the undervalue.

Example
A business asset with a market value of £10,000 is sold for £8,500. The asset was originally purchased for £6,000.

The actual gain is:	
Market value	10,000
—Cost	6,000
	4,000
But rollover is limited to:	
Market value	10,000
—Sale price	8,500
	1,500

128 Gift of Business Assets

Deemed cost to transferee:

Market value	10,000
—Rollover	1,500
	8,500

In other words, the actual sale price is used as the deemed cost of the recipient. Thus, £2,500 (4,000—1,500) is assessed on the transferor.

2. If the asset has been restricted in its business use, either during the time of ownership or the proportion of the asset used for business, then the gain which can be rolled over is restricted accordingly.

Example

Fred Cloggins bought a business property in April, 1970 for £8,000. He always used half of it for private purposes, and used it all privately for a period of four years. He gave it to a company in April, 1986 when it was worth £30,000.

Gain:	Market value		30,000
	—Cost	8,000	
	Indexation	2,000	10,000
			$20,000 \times \frac{9}{10} \times \frac{1}{2} = $ 6,000

Rollover:		
Market value		30,000
—Rollover		6,000
Deemed cost		24,000

Assessment:	
20,000—6,000 =	14,000

3. If the gift is of shares in a family company the rollover is restricted to the proportion of the gain that the chargeable business assets of the company bear to the chargeable assets of the company. A chargeable asset is one on which a gain would accrue on disposal.

Example

A man gives away shares in a family company to a company when they are worth £20,000. They had originally cost £6,000. The company's assets are worth:

Land and buildings	100,000 (showing a gain)
Goodwill	50,000 (showing a gain)
Plant & machinery	20,000*(showing a loss)
Stock	25,000+
Debts	15,000+
Investments in other company	
Shares	35,000 (showing a gain)
Cash	5,000+

Note: *The plant and machinery show a loss and therefore are NOT a chargeable asset.

Gift of Business Assets 129

+Stock debts and cash are exempt from capital gains. Therefore:
14,000 (20,000—6,000) × 150,000 (land & buildings and goodwill)

$$\frac{185,000 \text{ (land \& buildings, goodwill \&}}{\text{investments)}} = 11,351$$

Transferee's deemed cost
$$20,000—11,351 = 8,649$$
Chargeable to capital gains is
$$14,000—11,351 = 2,649$$

4. If a gain also qualifies for retirement relief then the rollover relief on the gift is restricted to the chargeable gain.

Example
Oldman gives shares to a company and qualifies for £50,000 of retirement relief. The shares are worth £80,000 on disposal and originally cost £20,000.

Total gain 80,000—20,000 =	60,000
—Retirement relief	50,000
Chargeable gain	10,000
Transferee's acquisition value	80,000
Chargeable gain rolled over	10,000
Transferee's deemed cost	70,000

Conditions

1. The transferor must be an individual and must dispose of the property to a person (other than an individual) resident or ordinarily resident in the UK.

2. Both the transferor and transferee must claim the relief.

3. The asset must be a business asset or shares in a family company. A "family company" is one in which the transferor can exercise 25% or more of the voting shares or at least 5% individually and his family have 51% or more of the voting rights. "Family" in this case means spouse, brother, sister, ancestor or lineal descendant of the transferor or the spouse.

Chapter Nineteen

Transfer of a Business on Retirement
(Ss.69, 70 Sch 20, FA, 1985)

Introduction

An individual retiring from business and transferring or selling his interest to someone else would be liable to capital gains tax on the disposal if it were not for retirement relief. The relief exempts gains of up to £125,000 (£100,000 up to 5th April, 1987) maximum on business assets, etc. disposed of by an individual who is:

1. Aged 60 or above; or,
2. Has to retire at an earlier age because of ill health which has made him permanently incapable of continuing to do the kind of work he did before retirement.

Prior to 6th April, 1985 the limit of 100,000 was only reached at age 65, building up at the rate of 20,000 a year from age 60. The ''ill health'' category was not available.

The relief is available on different types of disposal of assets.

Relief

Relief for disposals by individuals on retirement from family business
Relief is given when an individual makes a ''material disposal of business assets''. There are three of these.

1. A disposal of the whole or part of a business where throughout a period of at least one year ending with the date of disposal
   a) the individual owns the business he is disposing of; or
   b) the business is:
   i) Owned by the individual's family trading company (defined later) or by a member of a trading group of which the holding company is that individual's family company; and
   ii) The individual is a full-time working director (FTWD) of that company or of one or more companies which are members of the same group or commercial association of companies as that which owns the business.
   c) The disposal is of an interest in a partnership or of an interest in partnership business assets.

Transfer of a Business on Retirement 131

2. A disposal of business assets used in a business which has finished, when throughout a period of at least twelve months prior to cessation the business was owned by:

a) The invidual claiming relief; or

b) A company or holding company as described in (b) above.

The individual claiming relief must have reached 60 or retired on ill health grounds on or before the date of cessation and the assets must be sold within one year after cessation, or such longer period as the Board may allow.

3. A disposal of shares and securities in a company where throughout a period of twelve months ending with the "operative date" (defined below) either:

a) The individual owned the business which was then owned by the company or by a subsidiary company at the date of disposal; or

b) The company was the individual's family trading company, or the family holding company of a trading group and the individual is a full time working director (FTWD) of the company, or in the case of a holding company, an FTWD of any group company.

The "operative date" is usually the date of disposal, but there are two exceptions:

a) If within twelve months before the disposal the company ceased to be a trading company or member of a trading group, and the individual disposing of the shares reached 60 or retired because of ill health before the cessation, the "operative date" is the date trading ceased.

b) If the individual ceased to be a FTWD but continued as a director and worked on average at least 10 hours a week in a technical or managerial capacity until the date of disposal, or until the cessation of trading. Then the operative date is the date when the individual ceased to be a FTWD.

Relief for other types of disposals connected with retirement

Retirement relief is also available on the following three types of disposal.

Assets used in employment

When an employee makes a "relevant disposal" of assets used in his employment having attained the age of 60 or retired on ill health grounds, retirement relief is available.

A "relevant disposal" is one where the following conditions are satisfied:

1. The employment was full time for at least one year before disposal or for one year before he ceased work if he finished earlier; and

2. The employment was not as a director of a family company or of its subsidiary; and

3. When he ceased work before the disposal, he was 60 or retired because of ill health on or before the date he stopped work; and

4. When again he ceased work before the disposal that disposal takes place within one year of cessation of employment, or such longer period as the Board may allow.

132 Transfer of a Business on Retirement

Disposal of assets by trustees
Retirement relief is available when trustees dispose of trust property which is shares or securities of a company or an asset used now or previously in business, provided there is an interest in possession (not including one for a fixed term) and certain conditions are met:

For shares and securities the conditions are:

1. The company was the beneficiary's family trading company or family holding company of a trading group for at least one year ending not earlier than one year before the disposal. The Board can extend this period; and

2. The beneficiary was an FTWD of the company or a subsidiary for at least one year ending as in 1 above; and

3. The beneficiary ceased to be a FTWD on or within one year (the Board can allow longer) before the date of disposal, having reached 60 or earlier retired earlier because of ill-health.

For disposals of assets the conditions are:

1. The asset was used for a business carried on by a beneficiary throughout one year before the disposal (the Board can allow longer); and

2. The beneficiary ceased to carry on the business within one year (or longer if the Board allow) before disposal; and

3. The beneficiary reached 60 or retired earlier because of ill health on or before the disposal, or if earlier, the date of cessation of trade.

Assets owned by an individual partner or director used by the partnership or company
Relief can be claimed for disposal, or an asset owned by the individual but used by the partnership or company, if the disposal is an "associated disposal". Such a disposal takes place when:

1. It takes place in association with a withdrawal from the partnership or company; and

2. The asset was used for the purposes of trade until immediately before the individual's retirement, etc; and

3. The asset has been used for all or part of the time owned by the individual for business purposes, including other previous business use by the individual, a partnership or family company.

4. No rent has been charged by the individual. A charge of commercial rent means no relief at all, and partial relief if less than a commercial rent is charged.

Election for relief
No election need be made if the individual has attained 60, but in other cases (ill health) an election has to be made within two years after the disposal.

A claim for relief by trustees must be made jointly by the trustees and the beneficiary.

Transfer of a Business on Retirement 133

Gains qualifying for relief
First of all the property disposed of must be business property, and not merely an asset used in the business which does not have a significant importance to the business. In the case of McGREGOR v ADCOCK (STC 1977 206), a sale of surplus land by a farmer was deemed not to qualify for retirement relief.

When shares or securities in a company are sold only the "appropriate proportion" of the gain made qualifies for retirement relief. This proportion is:

1. For a trading company which is not a holding company, the proportion the company's "chargeable business assets" bear to the "chargeable assets."

2. For a holding company, the proportion of the trading group's chargeable business assets bear to the value of the group's chargeable assets.

If the company or group does not have any chargeable assets the appropriate proportion is the whole.

Every asset is a "chargeable asset" except those where any gain would not be a chargeable gain (stock, debtors, cash, etc.). They do include assets which are chargeable but not necessarily showing a gain at that time. A holding of shares by a holding company in a subsidiary is not a chargeable asset and also a chargeable business asset.

If a subsidiary company is not wholly owned, the value of its chargeable assets and chargeable business assets are reduced proportionately.

A "chargeable business asset" is an asset used for the business which is chargeable to capital gains if disposed of at a profit (e.g. plant and machinery may not be a chargeable business asset if it has a value less than £3,000 and thus is not a chargeable "chattel"). The definition is also intended to provide for use by a trading subsidiary of a family holding company, by a partnership and by a beneficiary using settled property in his business.

Example

Jerry Bilt has a 35% shareholding in Rent-a-Ruin Ltd. (purveyors of mock stately homes to the gentry). He retires at the age of 61 and shows a gross gain of £120,000 on the disposal of his shares.

At the time of disposal the company's assets are valued as follows:

Chargeable business assets:

Land & buildings used in trade	400,000	
Goodwill	100,000	
Plant & machinery (valued at over £3,000 per item)	50,000	550,000

Other chargeable assets:

Property let on rental	100,000	
Stock market investments	50,000	150,000

134 Transfer of a Business on Retirement

Non-chargeable assets:

Plant & machinery (valued at under £3,000 per item)	10,000	
Stock & work in progress	80,000	
Debtors	40,000	
Cash	2,000	150,000
Total assets		850,000

Gain qualifying for retirement relief:

$$120,000 \times \frac{550,000}{700,000 \ (550,000 + 150,000)} = 94,286$$

Therefore, 25,714 (120,000−94,286) of gain is taxable, subject to the annual exemption.

Disposals other than material disposals

Miscellaneous rules apply to disposals other than "material disposals":

1. When there is a trustee's disposal and another beneficiary other than the one carrying on the business (called the "qualifying beneficiary") also has an interest in possession in the same property, only a proportion, called the "relevant proportion" of the gain on the trustees qualifies for relief. This proportion is the same as the qualifying beneficiary's proportionate interest.

2. When the disposal is an associated disposal only part of the gain qualifies for relief if the asset was not wholly used for business purposes or for only part of the time, or used for a business with which the owner was not concerned, or rent was paid for use of the asset. That part which qualifies for relief is what seems just and reasonable to the Board after taking into account the relevant poeriods of business use and the amount of rent paid. Relief will only be given proportionately if less than a full rent is paid.

3. When a material disposal or a trustee's disposal is a capital distribution (see S.70) the gain qualifying for relief is restricted if chargeable business assets are included in the distribution. If the distribution is wholly of such assets, no relief is due, and is proportionately reduced when the distribution consists partly of such assets.

For the purposes of a capital distribution within S.70, the recipient can elect within 12 months of the distribution date for any asset sold within 6 months before the end of the qualifying period to be treated as continuing to belong to and be used by the company, and for the disposal proceeds not to form part of the assets of the company.

Amount of the relief

The maximum relief available is £125,000, but the proportion actually granted depends on the length of the qualifying period, which is a minimum of 1 year (10% relief) up to a maximum of 10 years (100% relief).

Transfer of a Business on Retirement 135

Example

Smart has been a FTWD of his family trading company, United Widgets Incorporated, Ltd. At the age of 61, having been with the company for 8 years, he disposes of 20,000 out of his holding 30,000 shares, making a gain of 110,000. On his 63rd birthday he disposes of the remainder of the shares, making a 70,000 gain.

Relief available:

First disposal − gross gain		110,000
Qualifying period 8 years = 125,000×80% =		(100,000)
Chargeable		10,000
Second disposal − gross gain		70,000
Qualifying period 10 years =	125,000	
Previously utilised	(100,000)	25,000
Chargeable		45,000

For this purpose a trustees' disposal is regarded as being made by the beneficiary. However, if the beneficiary at the same time makes a material disposal of business assets, the relief is applied to the material disposal in priority to the trustees' disposal.

If the qualifying period (the "original qualifying period") is less than ten years, but the individual or beneficiary was previously concerned in conducting another business earlier in the ten years, and there was a gap of no longer than two years between the two qualifying periods, the two are aggregated, but with a suitable deduction of qualifying relief for the gap.

Example

Rogers retires at the age of 60 in 31st May, 1987 having run the business since 1st June, 1982 (5 years). He had previously run another business from 1st June, 1975 until 31st August, 1980.

In the ten years (1st June, 1977 until 31st May, 1987) there was a gap of 1 year and 9 months (1.75 years). Therefore relief available on disposals at 31st May, 1987 is:

Gross	125,000
Restriction 125,000×17.5% =	(21,875)
Relief available	103,125

136 Transfer of a Business on Retirement

Assets received from spouse

When an individual makes a material disposal of business assets he/she inherited or received by way of gift from their spouse, he/she can make a written election within 2 years of any disposal for his own qualifying period to be extended by the spouse's qualifying period, provide the spouse fulfilled the relevant conditions.

However, when the assets were received on a lifetime gift, the relief is not to exceed the lower of:

1. 125,000 less any relief given to the spouse or on a trustees' disposal when the spouse was a beneficiary; and

2. The amount of relief assuming no gift had been made, and the spouse had contained the business i.e. the spouse's age (if younger) will be relevant in determining the amount of relief, as well as the length of the spouse's qualifying period.

Example

Amelia and Ernest Plackett have run a business in partnership, in which Amelia has been engaged for seven years, and Ernest ten years. Amelia retires at age 60, gifts her half share to Ernest, who retires one year later age 62, selling the entire business at a profit of 220,000.

Assumed:

		Chargeable
Ernest ½×220,000 =	110,000	
Relief available	125,000	Nil
Amelia ½×220,000 =	110,000	
Relief available 125,000×80% =	100,000	10,000
		10,000

Definitions

Retirement an ill-health grounds

The Board have to be satisfied that a person has finished the work previously undertaken, and is likely to remain permanently incapable of engaging again in that work by reason of ill-health. Production of reasonable evidence is required, and there is an appeal against the Board's decision to the special commissioners.

Family company

This is a company in which either:

1. The individual has at least 25% of the voting rights; or

2. He has at least 5% of the voting rights individually and together with his family (spouse, brother, sister, ancestor or lineal descendant of self or spouse) has at least 50% of voting rights.

The voting rights of trustees are included when the individual or any member of his family is as beneficiary of the settlement (to the exclusion of outsiders) and no outsider could become entitled under the settlement unless the individual or any of his family failed to become entitled.

Trading company and trading group
These are companies/groups whose business consists wholly or mainly of the carrying on of a trade.

Full time working director (FTWD)
This is a director required to devote substantially the whole of his time to the work of the company/companies in a managerial or technical capacity. If an individual has retired from full-time employment but continued to work for at least ten hours a week for the company since then, he still qualifies for retirement relief.

Commercial association of companies
An association of companies carrying on business of such as nature that all the companies taken together may reasonably be considered to be a single commercial undertaking.

Chapter Twenty

Business Assets — Miscellaneous Matters

The trading stock of a business does not generally enter into any capital gains computations as any profit on its disposal is of course assessed to income tax or corporation tax as a trading profit under Case I of Schedule D.

However, the capital gains aspects have to be considered on two occasions:

1. When a person who has acquired an asset introduces it into a business as stock in trade. When this happens there is a chargeable occasion. The value of the item is its market value at the date of disposal, and this figure is also the "cost" of the stock to the business. (S.122).

An election can be made to avoid any gain at this point, and if so the "cost" to the business of the stock acquired is its market value less any gain or plus any loss on the disposal. You must exclude, of course, any gain or loss arising before 6th April, 1965.

2. If a person takes the stock of a business for his own personal use (even on the cessation of a trade), the profit on the retail value of the goods will be assessed to Case I, Schedule D. No gain is assessable, but the acquisition price for any future disposal is the amount taken into account in Case I, Schedule D.

Liquidations

On the liquidation of a limited company there are two separate occasions on which capital gains tax arises:

1. Gains or losses accruing to the company on the sale or disposal of its assets by the liquidator.

2. Gains or losses accruing to the shareholders on the repayment of their share capital by the liquidator.

Even if the assets of the company are taken over by the shareholders in specie as payment for the shares, there are two separate chargeable occasions.

During the liquidation, shareholders often receive more than one distribution. Each distribution, other than the final one, is strictly a part disposal by the company, and the residual value of the shares should be ascertained in order to apportion part of the cost to the part disposal.

To get round this difficulty in the case of unquoted companies, the Inland Revenue are prepared to deal with the calculations on a reasonable practical basis.

Business Assets — Miscellaneous Matters 139

If the liquidation is expected to be completed within two years of the first distribution payment, the Revenue will accept any reasonable estimate of the value of the shares at the date of distributions. If the distributions are completed before any assessment is raised (and normally the Revenue will not raise any assessments for two years) the Revenue are prepared to accept the residual value of the shares in relation to any particular distribution is equal to the actual amount of the subsequent distributions.

Where time-apportionment applies, the Revenue are prepared to calculate the gain on each distribution by applying the fraction as at the date of the first distribution without any further adjustment.

When in the case of a close company income tax has been paid on an apportionment of relevant income by an individual shareholder, and has not had relief on the income tax paid, he can add it to the base cost of his share on any disposal.

Revision questions

1. The British Sludge Co. Ltd. bought a factory in May, 1976 for £25,000. This was sold for £28,000 in June, 1988, and the proceeds reinvested in a new factory in May, 1989, at a cost of £27,000 which was eventually sold in July, 1991 for £30,000 and not replaced.

How would the gains be dealt with if the company claimed rollover relief? Ignore indexation.

2. Bloggs bought a warehouse in May, 1987, for £60,000, and sold it for £80,000 in October, 1990. He replaced it in November, 1990 with a temporary shelter (estimated life 20 years) costing £140,000. This was itself sold in August, 1992 for £170,000 and replaced by a permanent structure which cost £120,000.

Rollover relief was claimed on both occasions. Work out the assessments and the various reliefs. Ignore indexation.

3. Bloggs converted his thriving business into Bloggs Enterprises Ltd. in June, 1987. The gains chargeable were £8,000. The company gave in consideration:

	£
Cash	10,000
Shares (market value)	30,000

Calculate the assessable gain on the transfer and the deemed price of the shares for any future disposal. Ignore indexation.

4. Fossil, an antique dealer, held a piece of silver as part of his private collection. He had purchased the silver for £3,000 in 1987. He appropriated it as part of his business stock in February, 1988 when its value was £4,000.

How could he have the silver treated to avoid a capital gain assessment in 1987-88?

140 **Business Assets — Miscellaneous Matters**

5. Fred Seagoon started a business in September, 1972 purchasing:

Factory	20,000
Plant & machinery	5,700
Stock	3,000

He sold the factory in May, 1982 for £48,000 replacing it the same year with one costing £45,000.

He transferred the business as a going concern (retaining the cash) to a limited company in June, 1987 in exchange for 50,000 ordinary £1 shares and 20,000 in cash. At the time the balance sheet showed these values:

Factory	62,000
Goodwill	15,000
Plant & Machinery	4,200
Stock	4,800
Cash	3,000
Debtors	6,000
	95,000
—Liabilities	22,500
	73,000

On reaching the age of 64 in November, 1988 he sold 10,000 for £42,000, having been a fulltime working director since June, 1987. The company balance sheet showed:

Factory	100,000
Goodwill	25,000
Plant & Machinery*	4,000
Investments in shares	30,000
Stock	8,000
Cash	20,000
Debtors	13,000
	200,000
—Liabilities	20,000
	180,000

*All items valued at under £3,000.

Work out all the potential and actual capital gains, assuming all appropriate reliefs are claimed, ignoring indexation.

Answers

1. First sale:

	£
Sale price	28,000
Less: Purchase price	25,000
Gain	3,000

Business Assets — Miscellaneous Matters 141

But only £27,000 reinvested in a replacement asset. £2,000 is therefore carried forward under the rollover provisions and £1,000 becomes assessable.
Second sale:

Sale price		30,000
Less: Purchase price	27,000	
Reduced by	2,000	25,000
Assessable gain		5,000

2. First sale:

Sale price		80,000
Less: Purchase price		(60,000)
Gain		20,000

Payment of tax postponed for 10 years etc.
Second sale:

Sale price	170,000
Less: Purchase price	(140,000)
	30,000

OR
Withdraw postponement claim and claim rollover relief on new asset.
Price of replacement is reduced to 120,000 − 20,000 = 100,000.

3. Assessable gain:

$$\frac{8,000 \times 10,000}{40,000} = 2,000$$

Deemed price of shares:	30,000
Less: Postponed gains	(6,000)
	24,000

4. Gain:

Market value on transfer	4,000
Less: Purchase price	3,000
Gain	1,000

Fossil could elect to miss the gain and treat the cost of the stock in trade as £3,000.

5. **Sale of factory, 1982-83**

Sale price of original	48,000
—Cost	(20,000)
Gross gain	28,000

142 Business Assets — Miscellaneous Matters

Gain assessed	48,000—45,000=			3,000
Gain to rollover	28,000—3,000 =			25,000
Cost or replacement				45,000
—Rolled over gain				(25,000)
Deemed cost for capital gains				20,000

Transfer to limited company, 1987-88
Gains:

Factory	62,000			
	—20,000	42,000		
Goodwill	15,000			
	— Nil	15,000		
		57,000		
Gain assessed	57,700	20,000	=	16,285
		70,000		

Cost of shares received:

Gross cost		50,000
—Rolled over 57,000—16,285	=	(40,715)
Deemed cost for capital gains		9,285

Sale of shares, 1988-89

Sale price			42,000
—Apportioned cost	$9,285 \times 10,000$	=	1,857
	50,000		
Gross gain			40,143

Retirement relief:

Maximum available	=	125,000

Gain to which it can be applied:

$$\frac{40,143 \times 125,000}{155,000} = 32,373$$

Therefore:

Gain assessed	40,143
	—32,373
	7,770

Chapter Twenty One

Interest in Land

The taxation of land transactions

Introduction

Over the years many attempts have been made to impose special taxes on profits from land. In recent years the following have occurred:

1. Betterment levy (and now abolished).
2. S.488, Taxes Act, 1970 (artificial transactions in land).
3. Development land tax, introduced as from 1st August, 1976 but now abolished.

This chapter deals with land in three sections:

1. Land with development value.
2. Land without development value, particularly leases.
3. The anti-avoidance legislation in S.488.

All these rules are dealt with in this part of the book, but before examining these in detail some definitions widely used in connection with land are defined below:

Freehold land is not defined in the Acts, but means the tenure of land without obligation of service or rent.

Lease means in relation to land any underlease, sublease or any tenancy or licence and any agreement for a lease, underlease or tenancy or licence and in the case of land outside the UK any interest corresponding to a lease. In terms of property other than land it means any kind of arrangement or agreement under which payments are made for the use of or in respect of property.

Land with development value (exclusive of development land tax) is land or an interest in land within the UK acquired before April, 1965 and its value on sale is boosted by permission to develop it under the Town and Country Planning Acts.

Special rules can apply to all three categories and the following chapters look at these.

144 Interest in Land

General rules of computation

The rules of computation are those applied generally to most other assets with two main exceptions:
1. Land owned at 6th April, 1965 which has development value.
2. Part disposals of land.

Land with development value owned on 6th April, 1965

With normal assets owned on 6th April, 1965 there is a choice as to the method of computing the gain. This is to deduct from the disposal value either the value at 6th April, 1965 or the original cost and assess a part of the resultant gain ascertained by application of the time apportionment formula. In the case of land with a development value the time apportionment formula cannot apply, the value at 6th April, 1965 must be used.

However, the gain cannot exceed that arising by deducting the original cost of the land, and if by comparing the two methods one gives a gain and one a loss, then there shall be neither a gain nor a loss assessable.

The valuation of land at 6th April, 1965 is a matter for experts, but generally means the price which the asset might reasonably be expected to fetch on a sale in the open market. Regard must be taken of special circumstances existing at 6th April, 1965 such as the occupation of the property by a tenant at that date, whereas on a later sale it might have been with vacant possession. The value of the property in 1965 would be depressed in comparison to the sale price. What matters is the conditions and circumstances of the property in April, 1965.

Part disposals of land

The Inland Revenue have issued a concession to ease the difficulties of computation on the part disposal of land (press release of 22nd April, 1971).

The result of this is that a part disposal can be treated as the sale of a completely separate piece of land, and valuations made accordingly e.g. at 6th April, 1965. Any reasonable valuation will usually be accepted by the inspector.

Of course, a taxpayer can always demand the use of the normal part disposal rules.

If there is a part disposal of land after fulfilling two conditions, the taxpayer may elect for special treatment (S.107).

The conditions are:

1. The value of the part disposed of does not exceed £20,000. The election cannot be made if all disposals of land in the same year have given rise to total considerations exceeding £20,000.
AND

2. The part disposed of is small in comparison with the market value of the whole before disposal. The Inland Revenue regard the part as small if it does not exceeed 20% of the market value of the entire holding.

Interest in Land 145

If the conditions are fulfilled, the owner may claim the consideration received be deducted from the allowable expenditure to compute any future gain, and NOT be treated as a disposal.

Example
Bartle acquired a piece of land for £10,000 in 1982. He sold two parts of it:
  1. The first price for £3,000 in 1987 when the value of the land retained was £27,000.
  2. The second piece for £7,000 in 1988 when the value of the land retained was £16,000.

Sale in 1987

Sale price			3,000
Cost 10,000 × $\dfrac{3,000}{3,000+27,000\ (=30,000)}$	= 1,000		
Indexation (say)		400	(1,400)
Gain			1,600

OR (at taxpayers election).
Sale price (3,000) being less than 20,000 (overall) and 20% of total value of all land at sale 6,000 (20% × 30,000).

Cost		10,000
Indexation to date		4,000
		14,000
Deduct sale price		(3,000)
Carry forward		11,000

Sale in 1988

Sale price			7,000
Cost 11,000 × $\dfrac{7,000}{7,000+16,000}$ = (23,000)	= 3,348		
Indexation (say)		335	(3,683)
Gain			3,317

Rollover relief not available as sales receipt 7,000 is over 20% of total value (23,000×20% = 4,600).

Carry forward remaining cost:	11,000
	− (3,348)
	7,652
Indexation (say)	766
	8,418

146 Interest in Land

If the land is compulsorily purchased and the market value of the land disposed of is "small" (less than 20 per cent of the value of the whole) the rollover relief mentioned above can be claimed by deducting the amount received from the cost carried forward. The absolute limit of £20,000 of maximum receipt is removed.

Relief on compulsory purchase (Ss.111 A and B)

When land and property is disposed of under compulsory purchase powers, and is replaced by other property, the gain on the disposal can be rolled over against the cost price of the replacement property.

The relief is not available if:

1. The property is disposed by the owner initially approaching the authority with compulsory purchase powers.

OR

2. The replacement property is a dwelling house which the owner uses at anytime as his principal private residence on the disposal of which the whole or any part of the gain would be exempt.

This provision applies to any disposal on or after 6, April, 1982.

Chapter Twenty Two

Development Land Tax

This tax was designed to tax the extra profit arising from the granting of planning permission (or the expectation that it would be granted) for a change in the use of land or buildings situated in the United Kingdom. The intention was only to assess this additional or "windfall" profit, not the rise in value attributable only to inflation or an increase in the demand for land with that present usage (the current use value).

Technically DLT was chargeable when there was a disposal of an interest in land situated in the United Kingdom (note: land outside the UK was not affected) by a person (individual, trustees, incorporated or unincorporated bodies) irrespective of where they were resident, and realised development value (RDV) accrued.

"Interest in land" was defined widely as any estate or interest in land (including buildings) together with any rights in or over the land, (including any right to affect the use or disposition of the land.

DLT was charged separately from and in addition to any other tax on the same disposal (income tax, corporation tax, capital gains tax). However, any profit assessed to DLT was given as a credit against the other tax to reduce the assessable profit or gain. Sometimes the calculation of this credit was more complicated.

The tax was abolished in respect of disposals taking place and projects of material development commencing on or after 19th March, 1985.

Chapter Twenty Three

Leases

(without development value)

General

These are the subject of special rules which depend on the combination of four things:
1. If the lease is disposed of by assignment.
OR
2. If the lease is newly created, or a newly created sublease.
3. If the lease has a remaining life of more than fifty years.
OR
4. If the lease has a future life of fifty years or less, even if originally it had a longer time to run, of which less than fifty years remains.

If a lease is assigned, the whole of an asset is disposed of (and therefore no Schedule A liability arises). If the lease had a life of more than fifty years on assignment the calculation of the gain proceeds according to the normal rules of capital gains tax. If it has fifty years or less to run it is a wasting asset and special provisions are used.

Where a lease or a sublease is created, this is a part disposal of an asset. If the lease is for more than fifty years it is not a wasting asset, and a formula much like the normal part disposal formula is used. If the lease is for fifty years or less, it is a wasting asset. All these special rules are examined in detail below.

Determination of the duration of a lease (Para.8, Sch.3)

The duration is normally the term for which the lease is granted, but it is deemed to end earlier in certain circumstances. These are:
1. When the landlord has an option to terminate earlier.
2. When it is unlikely the lease will continue beyond a certain date e.g. because the rent could then be increased.

Grant of a sublease out of an existing headlease with more than fifty years to run (Para.2, Sch.3)

There is a part disposal of an asset and the normal apportionment rules apply, but the value of the retained portion has to include the capital value at the date of disposal of any right to rent. The formula to apportion the original cost is:

$$\frac{\text{Original cost} \times \text{Price received for lease (premium)}}{\text{Total of:}}$$

Total of:
1. Price received for lease.
2. Capital value of rents receivable during the life of the lease.
3. Capital value (at the date of disposal) of the reversion of the property at the end of the lease.

Grant of a sublease out of a headlease with fifty years or less to run (Para.4, Sch.3)

Again this is a part disposal but there are two main differences from the previous type:
1. The lease is a wasting asset.
2. Because it has a life of fifty years or less part of the premium is assessable. Sch.A and has to be excluded from the computations considered here. How this is done is outlined at the end of the chapter.

The first problem means a special formula has to be adopted to determine the amount to be deducted from the original expenditure if there is any. The amount deductible is that which will waste away over the life of the sublease:

$$\text{Original expenditure} \times \frac{\begin{array}{cc} \text{Duration of headlease at} & \text{Duration of headlease at} \\ \text{time sublease is granted} & \text{time sublease will} - \\ \text{(converted to a \%)} & \text{(converted to a \%)} \end{array}}{\text{Duration of headlease at beginning of period of ownership (converted to a \%)}}$$

Example
In 1978 Clark acquired a 40 year lease for £2,000. In 1986 he grants a 10 year sublease for the same rent he is paying and a premium of £500. Schedule A and indexation are ignored.

	£
Assessable gain:	500
Premium	
Less:	

$$2,000 \times \frac{87.33 \ (30 \ \text{years}) - 72.77 \ (20 \ \text{years})}{95.457 \ (40 \ \text{years})}$$

150 Leases

$$2{,}000 \times \dfrac{14.56}{95.457} \qquad\qquad 305$$

Chargeable gain (subject to a deduction for anything
assessed Schedule A) $\qquad\qquad$ 195

The percentages are obtained from an actuarial table drawn up by the Revenue
and reproduced at the end of this chapter.

When the rent received under the sublease is greater than the rent payable
under the head-lease, the deductible expenditure is reduced by:

$$\dfrac{\text{Actual premium}}{\text{Notional full premiums}}$$

Example

A person acquires a 60 year lease on property for £10,000 in 1972. He occupies
it until 1987 when he grants a sublease for 10 years at a rent greater than the
rent he is paying for a premium of £1,500. The premium payable for the same
rent would be £2,000. Indexation is ignored.

$$\qquad\qquad\qquad\qquad\qquad\qquad\qquad\qquad £$$

Premium $\qquad\qquad$ 1,500

Less:

$$10{,}000 \times \dfrac{98.059\% \ (45 \text{ years}) - 91.981\% \ (35 \text{ years})}{100\%}$$

$$= \quad 10{,}000 \times \dfrac{6{,}078}{100}$$

$$= \quad 608 \text{ limited to } {}^{1{,}500}\!/_{2{,}000} = \qquad\qquad 456$$

Chargeable gain (subject to a deduction for anything
assessed Schedule A) $\qquad\qquad$ 1,044

When the sublease is only for part of the property, the allowable expenditure
is apportioned between that part and the remainder in proportion to their
respective values.

Assignment of a lease with more than fifty years to run

The normal rules apply, there is nothing special about such a disposal which is
a normal disposal of all of an asset.

Assignment of a lease with less than fifty years to run

This is a disposal of a wasting asset, and the amount of the original expenditure
to be written off is calculated in accordance with special formulae. These ensure
a low rate of write off of expenditure near to fifty years, accelerating as the
duration of the lease approaches extinction. In the formulae certain periods of
time are covered into percentages in accordance with an approved table, copies

of which are obtainable from the Revenue. The formulae are:

1. The original expenditure to be disallowed from the amount deductible from the sale price is:

$$A(1) \times \frac{P(1)-P(3)}{P(1)}$$

2. For any additional expenditure the disallowance is:

$$A(2) \times \frac{P(2)-P(3)}{P(2)}$$

Where:

A(1) is the total of the original expenditure.

A(2) is the total of the additional expenditure.

P(1) is the percentage (derived from the table for the duration of the lease at the beginning of the period of ownership.

P(2) is the percentage (from the table) for the duration of the lease at the time when any additional expenditure is reflected in the nature of the lease.

P(3) is the percentage (from the table) for the duration at the time of disposal.

Example

Keers owned a freehold shop which he let to Smith on 1st April, 1976 on a thirty year lease for a premium of £4,900. Smith incurred incidental expenses of £100.

Smith assigned the lease on 1st April, 1986 for £4,250.

P(1)=30 years=87.330%

P(3)=20 years (30-10)=72.770%

Expenditure to be excluded:

$$5,000 \ (4,900+100) \times \frac{87.330\%-72.770\%}{87.330\%} = 834$$

The assessable gain is then:

		£
Sale price		4,250
Less: Expenditure	5,000	
less	834	4,166
Chargeable gain		84

Or, the gain could be calculated by simply allowing the cost × $\dfrac{P(3)}{P(1)}$

Sale price	4,250
—Expenditure $5,000 \times \dfrac{72.77\%}{87.33\%} =$	4,166
Chargeable gain	84

152 Leases

If the duration of the lease is not an exact number of years, the percentage to be derived from the table is to be the percentage for the whole number of years plus one twelfth of the difference between that and the percentage for the next higher number of years for each odd month, counting fourteen days or more as one month.

Example
A lease is assigned with 10 years, 6 months and 21 days to run. The percentage for P(3) would be:

10 years =		46.695
Complete months	6	
21 days	1	
	7 months	
Add: $\frac{7}{12}$ths × 50.038% − 46.695% =		1.950
(11 years) (10 years)		48.645

Exclusion of premiums charged to income tax under Schedule A or Schedule D

When a lease is granted which has a duration of less than fifty years and a premium is charged, part of that premium can be assessed under Schedule A (if the recipient is a landlord). The amount assessed under Schedules A or D is equal to the amount of the premium reduced by one fiftieth for each complete year, less one, of the duration of the lease granted.

Example
Smith grants a lease of 10 year's duration for a premium of £2,000.

	£
Premium	2,000
Less: $2,000 \times \dfrac{9(10-1)}{50}$	360
Assessable Schedule A	1,640

The amount assessed to income tax is excluded from the capital gains computation in one of two ways depending on whether the new short lease is granted out of:

(i) A freehold or long lease (i.e. still fifty years or more to run when the sublease is created)

OR

(ii) Another short lease.

When a short lease is granted out of a freehold or longlease, the amount assessed to income tax is excluded from the premium received and also from the consideration in the numerator of the fraction.

Leases 153

Example

In 1980 Houseman acquired the freehold of property for £14,000 and granted a 15 year lease in 1984 in exchange for a premium of £8,000. The value of the reversion (including the right to receive the rents) is £12,000.

Assessable Schedule A:

	£
Premium	8,000
Less: $8,000 \times \dfrac{14(15-1)}{50} =$	2,240
Assessable Schedule A	5,760

Only £2,240 is assessable to capital gains tax as follows:

Part of Premium (8,000—5,760)	2,240

Less: $14,000 \times \dfrac{2{,}240}{\text{(cost of } 8{,}000 + 12{,}000 \text{ (value of}}$
acquisition)   reversion)

OR $14{,}000 \times \dfrac{2{,}240}{20{,}000} =$	1,568
Chargeable gain	672

When the sublease is created out of a lease with fifty years or less to run at the time it is created, the amount of premium assessable to income tax is deducted from the total calculated gain, but not so as to create or increase a loss.

Example

In 1979 Field acquired a 25 year lease on some property for £9,000 plus £320 expenses. In 1987 he granted a sublease for 7 years for a premium of £6,000.

Assessable Schedule A:	£
Premium received	6,000
Less: $6{,}000 \times \dfrac{6(7-1)}{50} =$	720
Assessable Schedule A	5,280

Capital gain:	
Full premium:	6,000

Less: Part of cost:

$$9{,}320 \times \frac{66.470\%(17 \text{ years}) - 46.695\%(10 \text{ years})}{81.100\%(25 \text{ years})}$$

$= 9{,}320 \times \dfrac{19.775}{81.100\%} =$	2,273
	3,727
Less: Already assessed Schedule A	5,280
Assessable capital gain	Nil

154 **Leases**

Actuarial table for leases

Years	Percentage		
50 (or more)	100	24	79.622
49	99.657	23	78.055
48	99.289	22	76.399
47	98.902	21	74.635
46	98.490	20	72.770
45	98.059	19	70.791
44	97.595	18	68.697
43	97.107	17	66.470
42	96.593	16	64.116
41	96.041	15	61.617
40	95.457	14	58.971
39	94.842	13	56.167
38	94.189	12	53.191
37	93.497	11	50.038
36	92.761	10	46.695
35	91.981	9	43.154
34	91.156	8	39.399
33	90.280	7	35.414
32	89.354	6	31.195
31	88.371	5	26.722
30	87.330	4	21.983
29	86.226	3	16.959
28	85.053	2	11.629
27	83.816	1	5.983
26	82.496	0	0
25	81.100		

Revision questions (ignore indexation)

1. Jones acquired a 55 year lease on property for £30,000 in 1980. He occupied it until 1986 when he granted a sublease for 12 years for a premium of £20,000 at a rent greater than he was himself paying. The premium payable to acquire the same level of rent was £25,000. What is the capital gains tax assessable?

2. Boggins acquired a 40 year lease for £2,000 in 1983. He grants a 20 year sublease to Davies for £3,000 in 1987 at the same rent he is himself paying. What are the capital gains tax and schedule A situations?

3. McMudd owned a freehold shop which he let to Smith on 1st June, 1982 on a 20-year lease for a premium of £6,000. Smith assigned the lease on 1st June, 1987 for £5,000. What is the capital gains tax payable by Smith?

4. Green took a 30 year lease on premises in 1980 for a premium of £7,000. He incurred capital expenditure on the premises in 1985 of £3,000, and assigned his lease to Brown in 1988 for £9,500. What is the capital gains tax assessable?

Leases 155

5. Black granted a 10 year lease on freehold premises he originally purchased for £6,000 in 1982 to White in 1987. The premium paid by White was £9,500 with no rent payable. The reversion is valued at £14,000. Work out both the Schedule A and capital gains tax assessments.

6. In 1979 Smock acquired a 20 year lease on property for a premium of £7,000. He also incurred legal costs of £200. In 1987 he granted a sublease for 8 years in return for a premium of £20,000. Work out both the Schedule A and capital gains tax assessments.

7. On 1st January, 1980 Boob acquired a 20 year lease for a premium of £10,000 and incidental costs of £100. He sold the lease on 1st January, 1987 for £9,000 with expenses of £300. What is the capital gains tax assessment?

8. On 1st March, 1981 Glamm acquired a 40 year lease for £15,000 with legal costs of £400 and sold it on 1st March, 1987 for £11,000 with legal costs of £200. What is the capital gains tax position?

9. On 1st July, 1979 Bilge acquired a 15 year lease for £25,000 with incidental cost of £500. He extended the premises for £8,000 5 years later. On 30th June, 1987 he sold the lease for £31,000 with incidental expenses of £300.

10. On 1st March, 1978 Goggle acquired a 30 year lease for £18,000 with incidental costs of £600. He extended the premises 4 years later at a cost of £2,000. He sold the lease on 28th February, 1988 for £16,000 with incidential expenses of £200.

In all cases ignore indexation.

Answers

		£
1.	Premium	20,000

Less: $30,000 \times$

$$\frac{99.675\% \ (49 \ \text{years}) \ - \ 93.497\% \ (37 \ \text{years})}{100\% \ (50 \ \text{years or more})}$$

$$= \frac{30,000 \times 6.16}{100}$$

$$= \frac{1,848 \times 20,000}{25,000} \qquad = \qquad \underline{1,479}$$

Chargeable gain (subject to any Sch.A deduction)

$$\underline{\underline{18,521}}$$

156 Leases

2. Premium received   3,000
Less: $2,000 \times$

$$\frac{92.761\% \ (36 \ \text{years}) - 64.116\% \ (16 \ \text{years})}{95.457\% \ (40 \ \text{years})} = 600$$

Gain			2,400
Assessable Sch.A	3,000		
Less: $\dfrac{3,000 \times 20 - 1}{50}$ =	1,140		
	1,860		
			1,860
Assessable capital gain			540

3. Sale price of assignment   5,000
Less: Expenditure   6,000
Less: $6,000 \times$

$$\frac{72.77\% \ (20 \ \text{years}) - 61.617\% \ (15 \ \text{years})}{72.77\% \ (20 \ \text{years})}$$

=	925	5,075
Loss		(75)

4. Sale price of assignment   9,500
Less: Cost of Lease   7,000
Less: $7,000 \times$

$$\frac{87.33\% \ (30 \ \text{years}) - 76.399\% \ (22 \ \text{years})}{87.33\% \ (30 \ \text{years})}$$

=	868	6,132
Less: Additional expenditure	3,000	

$3,000 \times$

$$\frac{81.1\% \ (25 \ \text{years}) - 76.399\% \ (22 \ \text{years})}{81.1\% \ (25 \ \text{years})}$$

=	174	2,826	8,958
Assessable gain			542

5. Schedule A:

Premium received		9,500
Less: $\dfrac{9,500 \times 9(10-1)}{50}$ =		1,710
Assessable Sch.A		7,790

Capital gains tax:
Part premium (9,500—7,790)   =   1,710

Less: $6,000 \times \dfrac{1,710}{9,500+14,000}$ =   437

             Assessable capital gain   1,273

6. Schedule A:

         Premium received   20,000

Less: $\dfrac{20,000 \times 7(8-1)}{50}$ 2,800

                Assessable Sch.A   17,200

Capital gains tax:

         Premium received   20,000

Less: $7,200 \times$

$\dfrac{58.971\% \ (14 \text{ years}) - 31.195\% \ (6 \text{ years})}{72.77\% \ (20 \text{ years})}$ = 2,748

                                          17,252

Less: Already assessed Sch.A.   17,200

                Assessable capital gain   52

7. Proceeds of sale   9,000

Less: Costs $(10,000+300+100)$ =   10,400

$\dfrac{10,400 \times 72.77\% (20 \text{ years}) - 56.167\% (13 \text{ years})}{72.77\% (20 \text{ years})}$ = 2,373   8,027

                      Capital gain   973

8. Proceeds of sale   11,000

Less: Costs $(15,000+200+400)$ =   15,600

$\dfrac{15,600 \times 95.457\% (40 \text{ years}) - 91.156\% (34 \text{ years})}{95.457\% (40 \text{ years})}$ = 703   14,897

                     Capital loss   3,897

158 Leases

9. Proceeds of sale   31,000
  Less: Cost of lease*   25,727
  25,727×61.617%(15 years)—35.414%(7 years)

$$\frac{}{61.617(15 \text{ years})} \quad = \quad 10,941 \qquad 14,786$$

Cost of extension**   8,073
8,073×46,695%(10 years)—35.414%(7 years)

$$\frac{}{46.695\%(10 \text{ years})} \quad = \quad 1,950 \qquad 6,123 \qquad 20,909$$

               Capital gain   10,091

$$*25,000+500+\frac{25,000}{25,000+8,000}\times300=25,727$$

$$**8,000+\frac{8,000}{25,000+8,000}\times300=8,073$$

10. Proceeds of sale   16,000
  Less: Cost of lease   18,780
  18,780×72.77%(20 years)—46.695(10 years)

$$\frac{}{72.77\%(20 \text{ years})} \quad = \quad 6,720 \qquad 12,051$$

Cost of extensions   2,020
2,020×64.116%(16 years)—46.695(10 years)

$$\frac{}{64.116\%(16 \text{ years})} \quad = \quad 549 \qquad 1,471 \qquad 13,522$$

               Capital gain   2,478

Chapter Twenty Four

Purchase of own shares by unquoted trading company

General (Ss.53 to 56 & Sch.9, FA, 1982)

Arising out of changes made by the Companies Act, 1981 and subject to certain conditions, a payment made by an unquoted trading company to a shareholder for redemption or purchase of its own shares may be treated wholly as a capital payment instead of as a distribution liable to advance corporation tax and the higher rates of income tax.

This treatment can be applied in two main circumstances:

1. When the shareholder has owned the shares for a minimum period and as a consequence of the sale to the company there is a "substantial" reduction in the shareholder's holding in the company.

2. When the purchase consideration is used to pay capital transfer tax charged on a death which could not otherwise have been met without undue hardship.

Conditions

Unquoted trading company
In both cases mentioned above the company must:

1. Be unquoted. A company whose shares are dealt in only on the Unlisted Securities Market is regarded as unquoted for this purpose. If the company is a partly quoted company it will not qualify even though the shares purchased are unquoted. A company which is a 51% subsidiary of a quoted company is also regarded as not being unquoted.

2. The company, or the group of companies taken together of which it is one, must have a business which consists wholly or mainly of the carrying on of a trade or trades. The holding company of a trading group will only qualify if it has one or more 75% subsidiaries, apart from any trade carried on by it, wholly or mainly of holding shares or securities in the subsidiary.

For the purposes of defining "trade" dealings in shares, land and futures do not qualify.

160 Purchase of own shares by unquoted trading company

Qualifying occasions
Only in the following two cases will the payment by the company for the shares be treated as a capital transaction and not a distribution:
1. The payment is:
a) For the benefit of a trade; and
b) not part of a scheme to avoid tax; and
c) the vendor satisfies certain conditions listed below.
2. The proceeds of the sale of the shares are to be applied to pay capital transfer tax on a death.

Benefit of a trade
This is not precisely defined in the legislation, but the Revenue are to issue a Statement of Practice and have said that it is "a motive test, was that the purpose of the transaction?"

It would seem that where the shareholder sells his entire holding the requirement may be satisfied. It would appear that the main circumstances where the provisions will be used in practice are where the shareholder wishes to leave the company because:
1. He is one of the parties in a boardroom dispute.
2. He wishes to retire.
3. There is the shareholding of a deceased shareholder which the family wish to dispose of.
4. A shareholder who invested purely for capital growth and now wishes to realise his investment.

Purchase money used to pay capital transfer tax on death
This condition requires:
1. Substantially the whole of the purchase money is applied in paying capital transfer tax on a death; and
2. that it is so utilized within two years after the death; and
3. The capital transfer tax could not otherwise have been paid without undue hardship.

It would appear that under the definition of "undue hardship" only sufficient shares will have to be so to realise the minimum required to pay off the capital transfer tax or the balance of the capital transfer tax which cannot otherwise be funded.

Administration
These provisions apply in theory from the 6th April, 1982 although it has only been possible for companies to purchase their own shares since the 15th June, 1982.

Application can be made to the Inland Revenue describing any proposed transaction and clearance obtained in advance. This is dealt with later.

Conditions to be satisfied by vendor

General
The vendor must satisfy three main conditions:

1. He must be resident and ordinarily resident in the United Kingdom. Trustees are regarded as so resident and ordinarily resident unless the administration of the trust is carried on outside the UK and the majority of the trustees are resident and ordinarily resident outside the UK. Personal representatives are treated as resident and ordinarily resident if the deceased was.

2. The vendor must have owned the shares for a minimum period which in most cases is 5 years.

3. When the vendor retains shares in the company his interest as a shareholder must be "substantially" reduced.

Minimum period of ownership
The minimum period is 5 years, but this can be reduced to 3 years in two cases:

1. When a shareholder acquired his shares under the will or intestacy of the previous owner.

2. When shares are sold by the personal representatives of a deceased person.

Previous ownership by other persons can be included in the two cases referred to above and also when the shareholder acquired the shares from a spouse provided they were living together at the time of acquisition.

When the vendor has made more than one acquisition of the same class of share in the company, previous disposals are identified with acquisition on a LIFO (last in first out) basis. This allows the vendor to have the maximum possible period of ownership in determining length of ownership when selling shares to the company.

Substantial reduction in interest
In most cases the shareholder involved will dispose of the whole of his shareholding in the company. If, however, he retains some shares, there must be a "substantial" reduction to qualify for the capital gains treatment. This substantial reduction is measured in two ways:

1. His numerical shareholding; and
2. His entitlement to participate in the company's profits.

Numerical shareholding
The nominal value of the shares owned by the vendor and his associates before the disposal is expressed as a fraction of the issued share capital of the company, and also his holding of shares is also expressed as such a fraction after the disposal. The fraction after the disposal must not exceed 75% of the fraction before the disposal. Thus, merely selling 25% or more of the original holding is not nearly enough. And, since all the share capital is aggregated, preference shares can prevent the test being satisfied, even if the entire equity holdings is disposed of.

162 Purchase of own shares by unquoted trading company

Example

Smalley owns 2,000 shares out of an issued share capital of 5,000 in Little & Large Ltd; an unquoted trading company. To achieve a "substantial" reduction he would have to dispose of 714 shares to satisfy the test:

a) Fraction of issued shares before sale $= \dfrac{2,000}{5,000}$

b) Target fraction after the sale $= 75\% \times \dfrac{2,000}{5,000} = 0.3$

Thus, the fraction will be achieved if the number of shares sold is at least 714.
Thus:

Shares sold

Fraction after sale $= \dfrac{2,000 - 714 = 1,286}{5,000 - 714 = 4,286} = 0.3$ 714

This amounts to a "substantial" reduction, but is 35.7% of the shares originally held (714 as a percentage of 2,000).

The minimum number of shares to be sold (714 in this example) can be calculated by using a formula:

$$x = \frac{a \times b}{4b - 3a}$$

When:

a = nominal value of the shares owned prior to disposal;

b = nominal value of the total share capital prior to the sale; and

x = the minimum number of shares to be sold.

Thus:

$$x = \frac{2,000 \times 5,000}{20,000 - 6,000} = \frac{10,000,000}{14,000} = 714$$

Distributable profits

The substantial reduction in entitlement to a profit assumes the company distributes all the profits available as defined in the Companies' Act, 1980 Part III plus £100 and the amount which would be needed to pay all fixed rate distributions for a year. If the payment by the company for the purchase of its shares exceeds the profit available for distribution immediately before the purchase, the latter is also increased by the amount of the excess. The comparison is that the fraction of which the numerator is the shareholder's share and the denominator is the total of those profits, immediately before and immediately after the purchase. The latter must not exceed 75% of the former.

Purchase of own shares by unquoted trading company 163

Association
If after the sale the shareholders "associated" with any other person who has shares in the company, then the "substantial" tests must be carried out adding the shareholdings of his associates to his own. There can also be a similar adjustment if the company purchasing the shares is a member of a group immediately before the purchase and the shareholder selling the shares is associated with any person holding shares in any company in the group.

"Associates" are defined as follows:

1. Spouses

2. A child under the age of 18 is associated with his parents.

3. A person connected with a company is an associate of the company or any other company controlled by it and any company and other companies controlled by it or his associates.

4. When a person connected with one company has control of another company the second company is an associate of the first.

5. When shares of a company are held by trustees (other than bare trustees) the trustees are associated with any person who provided property for the trust, any spouse or children under the age of 18 of that person, and any person who may be entitled to a significant interest in the trust.

6. Personal representatives are associated with any person who may beneficially be entitled to those shares.

7. When one person is accustomed to act on the directions of another then the latter are associated with that company.

A person is "connected" with a company if he is directly or indirectly possessed or entitled to acquire more than 30% of the issued ordinary share capital or the loan capital and issued share capital or the voting power in the company.

Groups of companies
For the purposes of determining the substantial reduction test where the company is a member of a group, a group is defined as being the parent and its 51% subsidiaries.

The group treatment applies in three circumstances:

1. Where immediately after the purchase the vendor owns shares in any other member of the group.

2. Where immediately after the purchase he owns shares only in one of the purchasing companies, but has owned shares in other companies immediately before the purchase.

3. Immediately before the purchase an associate of the vendor owns share in any other company in the group.

164 Purchase of own shares by unquoted trading company

No continuing connection
Immediately after the sale of the share the shareholder must not be "connected" with the purchasing company or any company in the same group. "Connection" is defined as:

1. He must not have control of the company as defined in Section 534, TA, 1970.

2. The power to ensure that the affairs of the company are conducted in accordance with his wishes whether by virtue of his shareholdings or voting or other powers in the company.

3. He must not own, either himself or with associates, more than 30% of the company's issued share capital, its loan capital and issued share capital taken together, or the votes in the company.

4. He must not have or be entitled to acquire by himself or with associates rights which would give him more than 30% of the distributable assets of the company on a winding up.

Administration

Advance clearance
A company can apply to the Revenue for clearance any proposed scheme it puts before the Revenue. The application must be in writing to the Board giving full particulars of the transactions and within 30 days the Board must either require further particulars or give a decision.

Returns and information
The company must inform the Inspector within 60 days of making the relevant payment.

The Inspector may require written information from the company or any person connected with the company concerning any scheme or arrangement of which the payment by the company forms part. The information must be provided within the period specified by the Inspector being not less than 60 days.

Advance corporation tax
When a payment made by a company is treated as a distribution the ACT payment may be surrendered to its 51% subsidiaries in the same way as ACT paid in respect of dividend.

Close companies – apportionment of income
A payment made out of distributable income by a close company for the redemption of its own shares is precluded from being a distribution for income tax purposes, but nevertheless has to be taken into account as a distribution in ascertaining the excess of relevant income to be apportioned amongst participators of a close company.

In applying the requirements of the company's business test the money used to purchase the company's own shares is ignored. Such money is treated as being available for distribution.

Dealers in shares

When a company redeems its own shares from a share dealer the payment to the vendor is treated as a trade receipt in his hands.

Chapter Twenty Five

The Anti-Avoidance Legislation
(S.488)

Land (S.488, TA, 1970)

The section applies to three categories of land (S.488(2)).

1. Land or any property deriving its value from land acquired with a view to realising a gain from disposing of it.

2. Land held as a trading stock.

3. Land developed with a view to realising a gain from disposal when developed.

The legislation also applies to the disposal of shares in a company which holds land as stock-in-trade, where there is any scheme of arrangement whereby the land is not disposed of in a straight commercial transaction. (S.488(10)).

The section is not to apply to any appreciation in the value of the land prior to a decision to develop it. The legislation is only out to assess under Case VI, Sch.D profits from development.

When the section does operate, the whole of the gain is treated for income tax (and corporation tax), as arising under Schedule D, Case VI for the year of assessment (or accounting period) in which the gain was realised. There are special rules for computing the gain. (S.488(3) to (10)).

On the whole, owner-occupied property is exempt from the provisions. (S.488(9)).

Deemed interest on certain securities

New provisions apply to transfers of securities after 27th February, 1986 to counter bondwashing, by treating interest on securities transferred as accruing on a day to day basis between interest payment dates with appropriate adjustments to the taxable incomes of transferor and transferee.

For capital gains tax, where the transfer is with accrued interest, the accrued amount is excluded from the transferor's consideration and the similar relief is excluded from the transferee's consideration when he disposes of the securities. When the transfer is without accrued interest the rebate amount is added to the transferor's consideration and a similar amount is added to the transferee's consideration when he disposes of the securities.

Chapter Twenty Six

Foreign Matters

Shareholdings in foreign companies (S.15)

A shareholder of any non-resident company (which would be a close company if resident in the UK) who is resident and ordinarily resident in the UK, and domiciled in the UK if an individual, is chargeable on the proportion of any chargeable gain made by the company.

There are exemptions:

1. If an individual shareholder's proportion of the gain is less than one twentieth, he is exempted.

2. Chargeable gains are not assessed which:

(a) Are distributed within two years.

OR

(b) Arise on the disposal of tangible assets or leases of property used for a business carried on wholly abroad, or the disposal of a foreign bank deposit for the purpose of trading outside the UK.

OR

(c) When the company itself is assessed on the gain.

The tax paid on the capital gain can be added to the cost of the shares of the foreign company, provided the tax is not reimbursed by the company.

If the company pays the tax on the gain, the shareholder is not assessed in any way (S.15(10)).

Beneficiaries of foreign trusts (S.17)

A beneficiary of a foreign trust can be liable to capital gains tax on a proportion of the gains made by the trust if:

1. The trustees are not resident or ordinarily resident in the UK.

AND

2. The settlor (or any one of them) is domiciled and resident or ordinarily resident in the UK, when the settlement was made or the gain arose.

AND

3. The beneficiary is domiciled and resident or ordinarily resident in the UK in the year the gain arose.

168 Foreign Matters

Rules are laid down as to how the beneficiary's proportion of the gain is calculated, especially in the case of discretionary payments.

If the settlement was made before 6th April, 1965 any beneficiary not entitled to any of the capital cannot be charged to tax.

In the case of a reversionary interest, any tax charged is not payable until the title becomes absolute or the capital benefit is obtained.

Miscellaneous points

Double taxation relief is given in much the same way as income tax.

If gains cannot be transferred to the UK because of foreign laws, the payment of the tax is delayed until the gain can be remitted. A claim must be made for this relief within six years after the end of the year of assessment in which the gain arises.

Chapter Twenty Seven

Further Revision Questions

For answers see Capital Gains Tax Teachers' Manual

Retail price index

Throughout all the following questions use the figures given in the table below. The figures for April 1987 onwards are estimates.

Assume RPI:

April 1987	101.00
May 1987	102.00
June 1987	105.00
July 1987	107.00
August 1987	110.00
March 1988	120.00

Assessment of individuals
A1

Mr. and Mrs. Potter have these results for 1987-88. Work out the capital gains tax payable:

(a) Mr. Potter purchased 1,000 ABC Ltd. shares for £900 in 1976 and a further 3,000 shares for £2,000 in 1977. He sold 1,600 for £10,000 in August, 1987. Their value at 31st March, 1982 was £3 each.

(b) Mrs. Potter purchased 1,800 DEF Ltd. shares for £3,800 in 1975. There was a rights issue of 1 new share for 3 held in 1977 at a cost of £1 per new share. She sold 1,000 shares for £2,500 in August, 1987. Value at 31st March, 1982 was £1.50 each.

(c) Mr. Potter purchased a piece of pottery for £1,900 in May, 1984 and sold it for £1,600 in September, 1987.

(d) Mrs. Potter purchased £4,500 (nominal) of 3½% War Loan on 1/10/78 for £2,000 and sold the whole block for £1,700 on 20/9/87.

A2

Mr. Gold has these deals in 1987-88. Work out his capital gains tax payable:

(a) He purchased 900 shares in XYZ Ltd. for £1,500 in 1975 and 1,500 shares for £2,600 in 1976. In July, 1983 there was a rights issue of 1 new share for 4 held at a cost of £1.30 per share. In May, 1987 he sold 2,500 shares for £5,000.

170 Further Revision Questions

The value at 31st March, 1982 was £2 each.

(b) He purchased a block of 6 flats for £10,000 on 6/4/57 and their value on 6/4/65 was £25,000. He sells 4 of the flats for £30,000 in April 1987, when the remaining 2 are worth £15,000. Value at 31st March, 1982 was £6,000 per flat.

(c) He purchased a vintage car for £1,000 on 6/4/35 and its value on 6/4/65 was £10,000. He sold it for £20,000 on 6/5/87. Its value on 31st March, 1982 was £16,000.

(d) He purchased a piece of jewellery for £2,700 in May, 1983 and sold it for £3,900 in August 1987.

Private houses

B1

A man buys a house in Manchester on 1st October, 1957 for £3,000. He lives in it up to 31st March, 1960 when he leaves to work in Glasgow. He returns to Manchester on 30th September, 1968 and lives in the house up to 30th September, 1981 when he leaves it to work in London. He never returns to the house and eventually sells it on 31st March, 1987 for £80,000.

The estimated value of the house on 6th April 1965 was £9,000 and on 31st March, 1982 it was £35,000.

What is the capital gain assessable on the sale?

B2

A man buys a house for £6,000 (expenses of purchase £300) on 1st October, 1964. He lives in it until 30th September, 1965 when he leaves to live in another house. On 1st April, 1968 he takes over the premises again, using two rooms out of twelve for exclusive business purposes and lives in the rest. He buys another house and moves into it on 31st March, 1986 and finally sells the original premises for £24,000 (expenses of sale £400) on 31st March, 1987, the premises having remained empty for the last twelve months.

The estimated value of the original house on 6th April, 1965 was £7,000 and £30,000 on 31st March, 1982.

What is the assessable gain on the sale?

B3

Smith bought a house in Manchester on 6th April, 1960 for £6,000 (expenses of purchase £250).

He lives in it up to 5th April, 1966.

He leaves to work in London on 6th April, 1966 to 5th April, 1972. Returns 6th April, 1972 and adapts 2 rooms out of 10 for exclusive business use.

He sells the house on 6th April, 1987 for £60,000 (expenses of sale £500).

Its value on 6th April, 1965 was £10,000 and on 31st March, 1982 it as £30,000.

What is the capital gain on the sale?

Further Revision Questions 171

Computation of gains
C1
Kemp buys a shop on 1st July, 1939 for £6,000 (expenses of purchase £150). He extended it on 31st March, 1955 at a cost of £2,000. The value on 6th April, 1965 was £11,000. He sold it on 31st March, 1987 for £65,000 (expenses of sale £400). Value at 31st March, 1982 was 30,000.

C2
A building was purchased for £20,000 in 1967, the land costing an additional £11,200.

The building was destroyed in 1986 and the land sold for £45,000 in 1987. The value of the land in 1986 was estimated at £28,000.

No compensation was received on the destruction of the building.

Work out the capital gain or loss in each case. Ignore indexation.

Rollover Relief
D1
Fidler bought a factory in July 1983 for £70,000. He sold it for £95,000 in August, 1986, and bought a replacement factory in July, 1987 for £84,000.

D2
Smith bought a factory for £100,000 in 1976. He sold it for £250,000 in 1980, buying a replacement for £270,000. This was sold for £410,000 in March, 1987 and not replaced. It was valued at £300,000 in March 1982.

D3
Jones bought a factory for £50,000 in 1969, sold it for £87,000 in February, 1975 and invested the proceeds in plant and machinery which he continued to own until 1987.

In each case, what capital gains are assessable and when?

D4
Fred Crickett is a shareholder in Clickclack Ltd., a private trading company. The shareholdings are as follows:

	Number of Shares
Fred Crickett	49
Florence Crickett (Fred's wife)	104
Frank Crickett (Fred's son)	70
Frances Crickett (Fred's daughter)	30
George Grasshopper	147
Gillian Grasshopper (George's wife)	100
Total issued shares	500

There is no family relationship between the Cricketts and Grasshoppers.

Fred Crickett purchased his 49 shares for £1,400 on 6/4/60. Their value on 6/4/65 was £2,200.

172 **Further Revision Questions**

On 6/4/82 he gives his entire 49 shares to his son Frank when they are valued at £5,600. Frank retains them until 6/11/86 when he sells his entire holding of 119 shares to George Grasshopper for £20,000. Frank had acquired his original 70 shares from his father by gift on 16/10/69 when they were valued at £3,900. Their value at 31st March, 1982 was £120 each.

Fred Crickett also on 6/4/82 gave Frank the freehold of the Clickclack Ltd. trading premises. Fred purchased them on 6/6/68 for £30,000 and has retained the freehold personally every since. The premises were valued at £78,000 on 6/4/82. Frank sold them for £83,000 to George Grasshopper on 6/11/86.

George Grasshopper sells the premises for £95,000 on 7/8/86 and purchases new premises for £92,000 on 6/5/87.

Work out the capital gains consequences for Fred (1982-83), Frank (1986-87) and George (1987-88).

Quoted securities

E1

Larkin buys ordinary shares in ABC plc. as follows:
1,000 shares for £500 on 9/5/81
2,000 shares for £800 on 17/10/82
There is a takeover bid by XYZ plc in April, 1987 on the following terms which are accepted:
1 XYZ share for 4 ABC shares held plus £2 in cash for each ABC Ltd. share held.
The value of the XYZ shares after the takeover is £10 each.
Both companies are quoted on the stock exchange.
What is the capital gain assessable, if any?

E2

Lord buys the following shares in Stately Houses plc:
3,000 shares for £2,000 on 7/7/63.
1,000 shares for £1,500 on 6/6/64.
Value on 6/4/65 was £1.75 per share.
4,000 shares for £7,000 on 8/11/79.
Value on 31/3/82 was £3 each.
He sold 6,000 shares on 11/7/85 for £30,000.
Assuming these are the only shares he has ever held, would he be better off making an election for pooling or not?

E3

An individual buys the following shares of Shambles plc:
400 shares for £1,200 on 1/4/67.
Value on 31/3/82 was £5 each.
200 shares for £1,500 on 9/7/84.
300 shares for £2,800 on 15/9/85.
He sells 700 shares for £9,000 on 20/5/87.

Further Revision Questions 173

E4

Gilpin acquires shares in Grotty Enterprises plc as follows:
600 shares for £3,000 on 18/2/80.
Value on 31/3/82 was £7 each.
900 shares for £7,000 on 7/5/85.
There was a rights issue on 10/6/86 when 1 new share for every three held was acquired for £2 each.
He sold 1,500 shares on 11/8/87 for 15,000.

E5

Burns has the following dealings in the shares of Firelighters plc:
Bought 600 shares for £1,400 in June, 1964.
Value 6/4/65 was £3 a share.
Bought 700 shares for £2,500 in October, 1978.
Bought 300 shares for £1,000 in November, 1980.
Value at 31/3/82 was £50 a share.
Sold 200 shares for £1,200 in April, 1983.
Bought 400 shares for £2,000 in May, 1984.
Sold 1,500 shares for £15,000 in July, 1987.
No election has been made regarding the pre-April, 1965 purchase.

E6

Fanshawe bought 1,000 shares in Lossmaker plc (a quoted company) for £3,200 in July, 1983 and a further 700 shares for £2,900 in May, 1984.

In July, 1987 there was a rights issue of 1 new share for each 5 shares already held, at a cost of £2.50 for each new share.

Instead of taking up the issue, Fanshawe sells them for £1,300.

The value of the shares after the rights issue is £4 each.

E7

In 1970, Smith purchased 800 ordinary £1 shares in Conglomerate Ltd. (a quoted company) for £1,300.

In 1971 there is a reorganisation of share capital.

Each share held is exchanged for one 25p ordinary share (quoted) and three 25p ordinary share (quoted) and three 25p preference shares (non-voting) with a fixed interest rate of 10%. The values of these on the first day of quotation were:

Ordinary shares	£1.20 each
Preference shares	80p each

In July, 1987 Smith sells 500 of the ordinary shares for £1.90 each. Value at 31/3/82 was:

Ordinary shares	£2 each
Preference shares	£1.40 each

What is the assessable gain in each case?

174 **Further Revision Questions**

Unquoted securities
F1
Varley has the following transactions in the ordinary shares of Swarbrick Enterprises Ltd., an unquoted company:

He bought on 1st April, 1960 500 shares for £1,000

He bought on 1st April, 1963 a further 300 shares for £700

The value of the shares on 6th April, 1965 was £1.75 each

He bought on 1st April, 1967 another 700 shares for £2,000

He sold on 1st April. 1987 1,200 shares for £12,000

What is the capital gain assessable? Their value at 31/3/82 was £4 per share.

F2
Platt has the following dealings in the shares of XYZ Ltd., an unquoted private company:

He buys 1,500 shares at £2 each on 6th April, 1955

Their value at 6th April, 1965 is £3.50 each

He buys a further 500 shares at £3 each on 30th September, 1966

He buys another 600 at £4 each on 30th September, 1970

He buys 2,000 shares at £5 on 30th September, 1983, and 200 shares at £10 each 19th October, 1984.

He sells 3,500 shares at £20 each on 6th April, 1987.

Their value at 31st March, 1982 was £4.50 each.

What is the assessable gain on the sale?

Comprehensive examples
G1
Fagin has the following transactions in 1982-83. Work out his capital gains liability for that year:

1. He purchased 2,000 shares in Conkers Ltd. for £1,700 in 1974. On 30/6/87 Conkers Ltd. is taken over by Acorn Ltd., offering 3 ordinary £1 Acorn shares (value of each share is £1.30) and 70p in each for each Conker share. He accepts the offer. Value at 31/3/82 was £1 each.

2. He purchased 3,000 shares in Leaf Ltd., a private company, for £1,600 on 6/4/60. On 6/4/75 they were taken over by Hazelnut Ltd. who offered 1,500 £1 ordinary shares (valued £2.50 each) and 4,500 £1 debentures (value £1 each) in Hazelnut Ltd. for each Leaf Ltd. share. The value of the Leaf Ltd. shares on 6/4/65 was 75p. He sells 800 of the Hazelnut Ltd. ordinary for £5,000 on 6/4/87. Value at 31/3/82 was £3 each.

3. He purchased a painting "Adam and the Figleaf" by Nuddi, for £700 in 1976. He sold it for £3,600 on 10/4/87. Value at 31/3/82 was £2,000.

4. He acquired the freehold of 10, Oak Avenue for £16,000 on 9/5/84. On 9/5/87 he grants a 20 year lease of the whole premises for a premium of £10,000 and an annual rent of £3,000. The value of the reversionary interest is £15,000.

Further Revision Questions 175

G2

Hiram Enfire Ltd. purchased an office block in 1968 for £60,000 and sold it in 1982 for £110,000. Also in 1982 they purchased a piece of land for £85,000 (legal costs 5,000) and began to build new business premises.

In the y/e 31/12/82 they spent (all after 31/3/82):

Building (1):

Foundations (for whole building)	5,000
Factory portion	35,000
Office portion	2,000

Building (2):

Foundations	3,000
Works canteen	9,000

In the y/e 31/12/83 they spent (the project being completed on 30/6/82):

Building (1):

Factory portion	70,000
Office portion	10,000

Building (2):

Works canteen	3,000

They also built a road to connect the two buildings at a cost of 1,800

They sold the entire site on 30/9/86 for:

Land	170,000
Building (1)	150,000
Building (2)	20,000
Road	4,000

There were legal expenses on the sale of £8,000.

Calculate the tax consequences of all the transactions particularly:

1. Rollover relief of original office.
2. Industrial buildings allowance.
3. Capital gains tax. Ignore indexation.

Index

Acquisitions, 38
Actuarial table, 154
Administration, 2
Agricultural property, 144
Amalgamations, 96
Anti-avoidance, 174
Appeals, 4
Assessments, 4
Assets restored, 69
Assignments, 18

Bankruptcy, 18
Bed and breakfasting, 81
Beneficiaries, 16
Betting wins, 24
Bonus issues, 87, 91
Business assets, 28, 127, 139

Calculations, 44
Capital allowances, 10
Capital distributions, 85
Charge to tax, 3
Chargeable assets, 24
Chargeable occasions, 38
Charities, 6, 25
Chattels, 31
Close companies, 56, 164
Commissioners, 4
Commodities, 31
Companies, 19, 21
Company amalgamations, 86
Compensation stock, 105
Compulsory purchase, 146
Computation, 44, 50, 78

Connected persons, 56
Conversion of business to company, 117
Conversion of shares, 92
Currency, 24, 32

Death, 39
Debts, 30
Decorations, 24
Depreciating assets, 125
Destruction of assets, 38, 72
Development land tax, 147
Development value, 143
Directors, 130
Discretionary settlements, 16
Disposals, 38

Election, 100, 132
Exchange of shares, 94
Executors, 12
Exempted persons, 6
Exemptions, 20, 24, 26, 39
Expenditure, 44

Family company, 136
Financial futures, 31
Foreign matters, 175
Freehold, 143
Full time working director, 137

Gifts, 15, 39, 65
Gilt-edged securities, 115
Goodwill, 125
Government securities, 25

Index 178

Groups (of companies), 21, 163
Guarantees, 69

Husband and wife, 9

Ill health, 136
Indexation (General rules), 47, 66, 70
Individuals, 8
Inheritance tax, 65
Instalments, 4
Interests in land, 143
Interest in possession, 14
Investment trusts, 115

Land, 143, 174
Land tribunal, 144
Leases, 143, 148
Life assurance, 25
Life interests, 17
Liquidations, 23, 138
Loans, 69
Losses, 8, 10, 15, 68
Losses prior to death, 15

Market value, 45
Marketable securities, 25
Material disposals, 130
Motor cars, 24

Negligible value, 69
Non-residence, 175

Options, 30

Part disposals, 144
Partnerships, 6
Payment of tax, 4
Personal representatives, 12
Persons chargeable, 6
Pool treatment, 76
Premiums, 152
Private residence, 26
Purchase of by own company, 159

Quoted securities, 99

Rate of tax, 7
Reconstructions, companies, 95
Reorganisation of shares, 86, 93, 106
Replacement of assets, 71, 123
Residence, 175
Retail price index, 59
Retirement, 67, 130
Returns, 2, 164
Reversions, 148
Rights issues, 87, 91
Rollover, 52

Sale of business/company, 67
Savings certificates, 25
Scientific research, 6
Separated couples, 29
Separation, 9
Settlements, 14
Small distributions, 97
Sole trader, 130
Spouses, 9
Stocks and shares, 76
Superannuation funds, 6

Takeovers, 96
Time apportionment, 58
Trading stock, 174
Transfer of assets, 22
Transfer of business, 117
Trustees, 15
Trustees in bankruptcy, 18

Unit trusts, 115
Unquoted securities, 77, 102, 159

Valuation, 77
Value shifting , 75

Wasting assets, 32